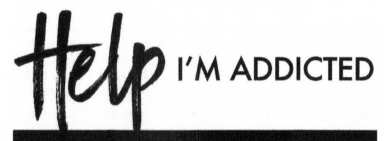

Help I'M ADDICTED

OVERCOMING THE CRAVINGS THAT OVERCOME YOU

Shane Idleman

El Paseo Publications

HELP! I'm Addicted: Overcoming the cravings that overcome you

Copyright © 2020 Shane A. Idleman

Editing and typesetting by Liz Smith of InkSmithEditing.com

ISBN-13: 978-0-9713393-9-2

ISBN-10: 0-9713393-9-2

Published by El Paseo Publications

Printed in the United States of America

Dedication &
Acknowledgments:

To my wife, Morgan—You have been a tremendous mother and wife. Your love and strength continue to amaze me. You are a true Proverbs 31 woman. Thank you for encouraging me in this endeavor—you truly are a blessing.

To my children—I pray that you make a huge difference in your generation.

I also thank my mother Diane Idleman, who has continued to offer guidance and encouragement. Not only is she a great mother but an exceptional editor and "book doctor." The nine books I have written so far would not be what they are today had it not been for her insight. I thank her for the many days, nights, weeks, and months invested—may it return a hundredfold.

Finally, this book is dedicated to all the families who have dealt with the pain of addiction. I hope that God will use this book to bring health, restoration, and deliverance.

Contents

A Quick Word to Pastors v

Disclaimer vii

Chapter 1: Addiction: Hope for the Hurting 1

Chapter 2: Changing from the Inside Out 9

Chapter 3: Resisting Temptation—The
Impossible Is Possible 21

Chapter 4: The Fully Surrendered Life 29

Chapter 5: The Cost of Addiction 37

Chapter 6: The Power of the Renewed Mind 51

Chapter 7: Overcoming Regret: Hope
for the Prodigal 59

Chapter 8: Pushing through Withdrawals 65

Chapter 9: The Gift of Health 73

Appendix 1: The Truth about Alcohol 87

Appendix 2: Depression and Mental Illness:
5 Things You Need to Know 95

A Quick Word to Pastors

We have a form of microwave Christianity. Service times are cut to just over an hour, prayer is glanced over, and worship is designed to entertain the masses. "People are bored," they say, "so our services need to be more appealing." You can increase attendance with slick marketing and entertaining programs, but you may miss the heart of God. The church will be a mile wide but only an inch deep. As Martyn Lloyd-Jones said decades ago, "Are we giving the Holy Spirit an opportunity? Are we so tied by our programs that He is excluded? Why this formality?"[1] These types of services will not help those in the throes of addiction or bondage.

To truly help people, we can have schedules for the flow of the services, but we shouldn't be clock watchers. Have worship, but allow God to move. Prepare a message, but be open if God desires to change it. Have a time of prayer, but don't be in a hurry. Why not go into worship and prayer and let people respond to the message? Breakthroughs cannot be rushed; we must spend time seeking God.

Why are a large portion of Christians in the West desensitized to strongholds in their lives? Why is there a general lack of conviction? Carnality not only affects the pew but the pulpit as well. A carnal pastor still offers motivating sermons, but he will lose unction, boldness, and spiritual insight. The

---

[1] Martyn Lloyd-Jones, *Revival* (Wheaton, IL: Crossway, 1987), 77.

world and carnal Christians will love him, but Spirit-filled believers will leave the service starving for more of God.

Pastors, if we would make it our goal to know Christ more personally, we would preach Christ more powerfully. Are we calling people out of the deceptive cultural mindset, or are we encouraging sin by our silence?

Disclaimer

This book was written based on personal experience and observation and is published with that understanding. The views expressed in this book should not replace professional medical advice. If professional assistance is required, the services of a capable authority are recommended. The purpose of this book is to motivate, educate, and encourage success. The publisher, *El Paseo Publications,* and the author shall be neither responsible nor liable to any person or entity with respect to damage caused, indirectly or directly, from the information provided in this book.

Information and website links are current up to the printing date. Neither the author nor the publisher endorses all the references from outside sources in this book. Related sermon links are provided for eBook users—simply click the embedded sermon link. If you are reading the printed version of this book, you will need to manually input the link into your browser the next time you are online. Some of the content from this book has been pulled from Shane's other books.

You knew this would happen.

How many times were you told?

But you challenged my power.

You chose to be bold.

You could have said "no,"

and then walked away.

If you could live that day over,

now what would you say?

—Unknown Author

1

Addiction: Hope for the Hurting

We are at a crossroads. Opioid and alcohol abuse are leaving a path of destruction in their wake. Pornography is desecrating families. Obesity is skyrocketing—plaguing millions and reaching epidemic levels in children. Heart disease and cancer are, by far, the leading "killers" in America.[1] And on and on it goes, from nicotine to caffeine to food. As a society, we are out of control. But are there answers? Yes, there are, if we once again set our sights on God's truth.

How can one book address opioids, alcohol, pornography, caffeine, gluttony, and all other forms of addiction? Wouldn't each need a volume of their own? While each addiction can be elaborated on, at the heart of addiction rests a common denominator known as a *stronghold*. This book focuses on weakening the strongholds in your life.

Addiction truly is hell on earth—you're enslaved but desperately want freedom, you're bound but can't break free,

---

[1] Murphy, Xu, Kochanek, Arias, "Mortality in the United States, 2017," Centers for Disease Control and Prevention, November 2018, https://www.cdc.gov/nchs/data/databriefs/db328-h.pdf.

you're in tremendous pain but can't find relief. If you can relate, don't worry, there is hope. If you feel you "just can't quit," I believe that you can. There *is* hope for the hurting.

BELIEVING A LIE IS ALWAYS THE FIRST STEP IN THE WRONG DIRECTION.

I have been addicted to many things, from coffee to sugar to alcohol, but alcohol was the most dangerous for me. I learned this lesson the hard way. When I first quit drinking, I stayed away from it for years. Then I thought I could drink on special occasions because it didn't seem to be an issue for me anymore. But because of my problem with alcohol as a young adult, the addiction was ready to take hold of me again. It took a few embarrassing situations for me to finally realize that my supposed "liberty" was really waking a dormant addiction.

Some days the desire to drink was difficult—it would last for hours until I finally surrendered to the temptation. The more I surrendered, the stronger the desire would become. Complacency led to apathy and, eventually, to compromise. I would rationalize, *Others are doing it, why can't I?* This mindset kept leading to failure. Believing a lie is always the first step in the wrong direction. I began to think, *If God really loved me, He wouldn't let me do this*, or *I've had a hard day. I deserve to relax.* Excuses kept me in a cycle of defeat, failure, and shame.

It was one of the darkest periods of my life. I was quickly losing hope. "God, please take this away," was my weekly cry. After finally hitting a low point, I began to seek God fervently and unconditionally. I asked a friend who had been through it before for help. His advice was simple yet life-changing: "You say no and let God handle the rest."

I realized that I had to cooperate in the process of change, avoiding people and places that triggered the addiction. And I had to confess my sin and repent of it. The common denominator in all my problems was *me*. Charles Spurgeon rightly noted, "We are never, never so much in danger of being proud as when we think we are humble."[2] We all must beware of pride and false humility.

I told a few trusted friends about my struggle and, although it was difficult, apologized to those who had been affected by my decisions. Pride is at the heart of addiction and must be crushed. Honesty, transparency, prayer, and disclosure are essential. Sin grows in darkness and loves the cover of night. Once exposed, it loses much of its power. While confession to others was humiliating and embarrassing, a great load was lifted. However, the struggles didn't immediately vanish.

I also had to put an end to compromise. Saying, "I'll just have one," tripped me up every time. I was doing the same thing but expecting different results—the classic definition of insanity. But when I focused on humility and accountability and decided to fight the demonic influences rather than succumb to them, victory was no longer elusive. I conceded that only God could change me. Full surrender is not optional. In this battle, we must surrender to win.

Once I did my part, God did His. By God's grace, He stopped the train before the wreck. Quitting was not easy, and the desire to drink did not leave right away. It was a battle, and anyone who has been there knows that. The first thirty

---

[2] Charles Spurgeon, "Humility," The Spurgeon Center, accessed October 10, 2019, https://www.spurgeon.org/resource-library/sermons/humility#flipbook.

days, for example, can be extremely difficult. But don't give up—look up.

Important Recap: Regardless of what your stronghold is, the points just mentioned are critical to success. Let's briefly revisit them:

1. Remove excuses.
2. Avoid triggers.
3. Own it and repent.
4. Apologize and repair the damage.
5. Crush pride before it crushes you.
6. Don't entertain compromise.
7. Admit your dependence on God, and fully surrender to Him.

Why wait? The train wreck could be just around the bend.

Sober but Not Saved

The most successful recovery groups are those built on biblical principles such as confession, repentance, and humility—admitting that we are powerless over addiction and realizing only God can restore us to sanity. We must decide to turn our lives completely over to Him (full surrender). We also must admit that our lifestyle is wrong and, when possible, make amends with those we have injured (humility and repentance).

I thank God for recovery groups, but unless a person turns to the one true and living God, they will be sober but not saved. We can't just say, "God, as I understand Him," or "a Higher Power"—we must confess Him as Lord and Savior. He is our only hope.

This really hit home for me some time ago. I had the privilege of attending a recovery meeting while doing research for this book. The guest speaker had over twenty years of sobriety, but she was suicidal, depressed, and confused; early childhood abuse had left her broken and shattered. Instead of offering listeners hope, her message was downright depressing. She was mad at God and made sure we all knew it. My heart truly broke for her—she was sober but not saved. This event motivated me to complete this book and help others find freedom and wholeness, not just sobriety. What does it profit us to gain the world [or find sobriety] yet lose our soul (Mark 8:36)?

We hear a great deal about God's judgment and what can keep us from heaven, and rightly so, because "the fear of the Lord is the beginning of knowledge" (Proverbs 1:7). But we also need to reflect on God's goodness, love, mercy, and grace.

Jesus healed my brokenness and restored my life, and He can do the same for you. A deep longing is inside all of us that cannot be satisfied until we recognize our need for a Savior, repent of our sin, and turn to Him. Once you do this, your past is forgiven, your present secure, and your future certain. Through Christ, you are a brand-new person. If you truly grasp this truth, it can motivate and encourage you beyond measure. Though the road ahead may be uncertain at times, the solid ground beneath will never shift. It's all about *Who* you know. (The next chapter will go into more detail on this.)

Childhood Trauma: Stepping-stone or Stumbling Block?

I've been told that I have a form of post-traumatic stress disorder (PTSD) because of suffering in early childhood from an angry father. This allowed me to excuse my actions for many years. I loved my father, who is now deceased, and appreciated his work ethic learned on the farms of Oklahoma, but he also brought a lot of anger into our family.

His addiction to caffeine and nicotine—along with being an unbeliever—was a big part of the problem. Our house was like a volcano waiting to erupt. When people use the phrase "walking on eggshells," I know exactly what they mean. To deal with the pain, I took my first drink at twelve then began drinking consistently around the age of sixteen.

I also used food for comfort and began to gain weight early on. I still remember the headline underneath my picture in our junior-high yearbook: *Stuffed Pig*. I was in a red wagon, with an apple in my mouth, being pulled around because I had just broken my leg. This was the triggering factor for my future steroid use and weightlifting; I shot up past 270 pounds and was bench-pressing over 400 pounds in my early twenties. My "I'll show you" mentality fueled this lifestyle of destruction.

As a child, I tended to isolate myself to prevent future pain. I became an approval seeker; something you would find hard to believe if you heard my preaching. Angry people scare me, and personal criticism hurts more deeply than it should. To my knowledge, my father never told me he loved me, but I know he did. He died at the early age of fifty-four.

The deep pains of childhood can follow us, and the enemy of our soul will use them against us. Thankfully, God makes provision for all our needs through His Word. He must be our anchor and our true source of hope. However, those who are enslaved often do the reverse—they turn to the addictive substance rather than to God. *One of the greatest lessons I learned is that we can either fully yield to God or we can yield to sin.* We are not robots on autopilot. We have been given the enormous responsibility of choice, and we must be accountable to our actions. We make a choice, then the choice makes us.

I want to pause for a moment and use this opportunity to speak to the parent caught in addiction. God loves you and wants you to turn from your destructive lifestyle. The choices you make today will dramatically impact your kids in the future (as well as your physical and spiritual health). Sadly, many babies are born addicted to opioids and will experience painful withdrawals. The cycle of addiction must stop, and it begins with you.

Don't let past pain continue to pull you down; use it as a stepping-stone. It's been said that shepherds from time to time would break the leg of a lamb that continually wandered from the flock and the shepherd's protection. The shepherd would then splint the broken leg and carry the lamb on his shoulders for weeks until the leg healed. As painful as this was for the lamb, it was necessary to protect it from being ravished by wolves or other predators. In time, through the dependent relationship, the lamb learned to walk and remained in the protective presence of his shepherd.

This concept was well stated by David in Psalm 51:8: "That the bones You have broken may rejoice." And Isaiah reminds us, "All we like sheep have gone astray" (Isaiah 53:6). Ironically, many thank the Lord for using their addiction to bring them back to the Good Shepherd. The lesson is to run to Him, not away from Him. Often, the greater the brokenness, the greater the dependence on God. *Those who have been forgiven much, love much* (Luke 7:47). Again, use past pain as a stepping-stone toward a closer relationship with God rather than a stumbling block that leads back to addiction.

One of the greatest joys associated with pastoring is seeing others filled with the Spirit of God: "You will seek Me and find Me, when you search for Me with all your heart" (Jeremiah 29:13). My goal is to fan the flames of passion toward God. This book is not a step-by-step guide written from a medical perspective; it's a biblically centered resource pointing you to the One who has the answers. As a pastor, I have seen the devastation that addiction brings, but I have also seen the victories: "Just as water ever seeks and fills the lowest place, so the moment God finds you abased and empty, His glory and power flow in."[3]

Take it further: For additional help, search for topical sermons at either WCFAV.org or ShaneIdleman.com.

---

[3] Andrew Murray, *Humility* (Nashville: B&H, 2017), 34.

2

Changing from the Inside Out

There was a man with the job of raising and lowering a drawbridge so passenger trains could cross a deep canyon. This man had one child, a son, whom he loved very much. One day the little boy wandered toward the bridge without his father noticing. Soon the father heard a train whistle. As he started to pull the lever to lower the bridge, he looked out the window and saw that his son had crawled down into the heavy gears. If he pulled the lever, his son would be crushed! There were only seconds to decide. Hundreds of people would die if he didn't lower the bridge—all sons and daughters loved by someone. He took a deep breath, and with his heart screaming with pain, pulled the lever. The bereaved father stood helplessly at the window, beating on it with both fists and screaming out in anguish, as the train zipped quickly over the bridge. The passengers thought he was waving, so they waved back, smiling and content, without realizing the price that the father had just paid for them.[1]

---

[1] "The Drawbridge Keeper," a version of a short story published in 1967, "To Sacrifice a Son: An Allegory" by Dennis E. Hensley.

This story has been shared countless times. It's a timeless allegory demonstrating the tremendous love God has for us and how we can truly change from the inside out. Sadly, many people are embarrassed to share this life-changing message because it may hurt their marketability. But shouldn't we be more concerned about credibility than marketability?

Choosing to change from the inside out is the most important step you can take. To truly change behavior, the heart must change. God promises deliverance if we turn to Him. D. L. Moody once said, "There is no peace until we see the finished work of Jesus Christ—until we can look back and see the Cross of Christ between us and our sins."[2] Are you heading in the right direction? If not, consider who or what is leading you—religion or a relationship with God.

- Religion says, "I have to follow rules." A relationship with Christ says, "Because of the price He paid for me, I want to follow His plan for my life."
- Religion says, "I have to go to church." A relationship with Christ says, "I want to position myself to learn more, worship Him, and benefit from fellowship."
- Religion lacks assurance; a relationship with Jesus offers unfailing guidance and assurance.
- Religion is man's attempt to reach God; a relationship with Christ is God reaching down to man.

No matter what you've done or have been through, you can repent and return to Him. A true measure of a person is not who they were but who they will become. Acknowledge that you are a sinner in need of a Savior (Romans 3:23).

---

[2] D. L. Moody, *Grace, Prayer, and Work* (n.p.:Morgan and Scott, 2016), 48.

Acknowledge that Jesus died for your sins (John 3:16). Repent and turn from your sins (Acts 3:19). Live your life for Him, not you (Hebrews 12:1–2). Live for Him. Trust Him. Serve Him. This is how we truly change from the inside out. It's important to begin with the right foundation: Jesus is the only way, the only truth, and the only life (John 14:6). When you hit rock bottom, look to the Rock.[3]

We Need a Wake-up Call

When my oldest daughter was very young, she nearly died in a drowning accident. While my wife and I were engaged in a casual conversation by the pool, my daughter walked down the steps and into the water. She was just a few feet away, yet we didn't notice her. Seconds later, my wife saw her struggling in the water, ran over, and immediately pulled her out. We thanked God for His grace that afternoon.

In the same way, sin works in stealth mode. It must be taken seriously, as it separates us from God and opposes His will. Sin corrupts our character and often leads us down the path of addiction. This is why so many Christians continue to fall backward instead of moving forward, working out their salvation with fear and trembling (Philippians 2:12).

I heard a story about a young boy who kept falling out of his bed while he slept. Frustrated, he asked his mother why he did that. She wisely answered, "It's because you don't stay far enough in." In the same way, many of us fall back into sin because we don't get far enough into God's covering of safety and protection. We also don't view sin as a serious infraction

---

[3] For more on this, watch the sermon "God's Scandalous Love" on YouTube at https://www.youtube.com/watch?v=6eJoZqNUysE.

11

against God. Romans 3:23 says that "all have sinned and fall short of the glory of God." Romans 3:10–11 adds, "There is none righteous, no, not one; there is none who understands; there is none who seeks after God." We all sin and fall short—no one is innocent. Humility recognizes that we are fallible human beings who have sinned against God. His Word is a lifeline to our soul, an anchor for our lives, not something to be debated, altered, or misrepresented. We don't change truth—truth changes us.

Imagine if a family member were stabbed to death with a knife and the police gave you the knife. Would you put it in the kitchen with the other knives? No, you would get rid of it or burn it. The same thing holds true with sin. We must view it as the weapon that destroys our lives, marriages, families, and nation.

Be encouraged—we all struggle with something. Like the apostle Paul in Romans 7:24, we must ask ourselves, "Who will free me from the domination of sin in my life?" Romans 6:16 answers, "Whatever you choose to obey becomes your master." We can choose sin, or we can choose to obey God. It's a choice.

In war, key battles must be won to assure victory. Today, absolute truth is one such battle. A weapon of relativism (man doing what is right in his mind) has set its sights on our nation, our homes, and our families. Our culture continues to challenge truth but to its own destruction. Attacking absolute truth is waging war on God. Unfortunately, Christians who sound the alarm are often categorized as irrational, judgmental, bigoted, and intolerant. But how can we warn if we will not confront, and how can we correct if we won't challenge? We are not called to make truth tolerable but to make it clear. If you truly want to change from the inside out, you must embrace God's truth.

Why is the world offended by the truth? Why are so many disturbed when the name of Jesus is mentioned? Why is His name, above all others, often taken in vain? The answer is simple: there is power in His name and in the cross—power that shakes the spiritual realm. Philippians 2:9–11 says that "God has also highly exalted [Jesus] and given Him the name which is above every name; that at the name of Jesus every knee should bow . . . and that every tongue should confess that Jesus Christ is Lord."

Sin and *repentance* have never been popular terms, even though they are at the heart of true change. Jesus Himself said that these things would be offensive. Sadly, many today water down the gospel and avoid difficult truths. They want the Bible to be more appealing and marketable, but truth is not marketable. We are to guard it, proclaim it, and defend it but never compromise it.

A skewed view of truth often leaves people confused and deceived because they believe in a self-promoting, self-seeking Christianity that bears no resemblance to Jesus's sobering call to full surrender. Jesus didn't say, "Follow me, and you won't have to change anything"; He said, "Deny yourself, pick up your cross, and follow Me" (Matthew 16:24). Jesus wants us to understand what's involved when we follow Him—there is a cost. The cross cost Him, and it will cost us too.

> A SKEWED VIEW OF TRUTH OFTEN LEAVES PEOPLE CONFUSED AND DECEIVED.

If current statistics hold true, many will continue to embrace a glamorized Christianity and be led astray. Life is a battleground, not a playground! If you've never sincerely repented and trusted in Jesus Christ as your Lord and Savior, this must be the first step. Yes, there are those who have overcome addictions by sheer willpower and motivation, but they are often not truly free. Many lack hope, peace, and assurance; but "if the Son makes you free, you shall be free indeed" (John 8:36)—free of guilt, shame, bondage, and addiction.

Many who are trapped in addiction go through life lacking passion, direction, and purpose, often living with a sense of remorse and guilt. A relationship with Christ changes that. Second Corinthians 5:17 states, "Therefore, if anyone is in Christ, he is a new creation; old things have passed away; behold, all things have become new." While there are consequences for past mistakes, it's better to live in God's arms redeemed rather than to live broken outside of His will. Which way will you run?

Choosing to change from the inside out is the first and most important step. But there is a battle; it is warfare. It's time to wake up and fight.

Does God Help Those Who Help Themselves?

The following analogy may help you understand the bondage of a stronghold. A pig and a lamb both find their way to the mud. The mud represents the sin that we all fall into. The pig wallows in and enjoys the mud and may even lead others in, whereas the lamb hates its condition and cries out. That's the difference—do you stay in the mud, or do you turn to God and allow Him to cleanse and redeem?

Encouragement is a great motivator, and while there is great encouragement in the Scriptures, there are warnings too. Though God is abounding in grace, we don't want to abuse His grace or test His patience. "Let go and let God" is a partial truth. Those wanting to lose weight can't say, "I'm going to let go and let God" while sitting on the couch eating donuts. Spouses can't say, "I'm going to let go and let God work on my marriage" and yet remain bitter, scornful, and resentful. And those addicted can't simply say, "I'm going to simply let go and let God," without also applying the principles found in His Word.

There is a middle ground between our responsibility and God's role in changing us. We have responsibilities, yet we are totally dependent on God. We must do our part, but we can't do His. It is God who makes us stand firm in Christ, but we must stay anchored to the Rock (2 Corinthians 1:21). We must fill our hearts with the things of God. We also must expose the addiction, install safeguards, and avoid the sin triggers. Change is not easy; it takes deliberate preparation. When we see something we need, desire, or want, our first impulse is to act on it. This defining moment is often the most difficult when overcoming temptation.

Second Corinthians 10:3–5 is crystal clear that we have responsibilities. It says that "the weapons of our warfare are not carnal but

CONTROL YOUR THOUGHTS, OR THEY WILL CONTROL YOU.

mighty in God for pulling down strongholds." It adds that we are to remove anything in our mind that goes against God. We are called to bring every thought into captivity to the obedience of Christ. In other words, control your thoughts, or they will control you.

Nevertheless, temptation is also an opportunity to grow spiritually and do what is right by turning from it. Being tempted isn't sin, surrendering to it is. The door of temptation swings both ways—you can enter or exit. If we choose to enter, once inside we may not see the exit sign so clearly again. Sin never stands still; it either grows or withers. Dan Delzell, in a riveting article entitled "Google Executive's Tragic Death Sends Somber Warning," wrote the following: "How do you go from being a devoted father of five and a successful Silicon Valley executive, into a 51-year-old man convulsing from a fatal dose of heroin on your 50-foot yacht, with a prostitute walking over your dying body to take a final sip of wine before leaving you to die?" He then presented the question, "How can such a tragedy take place?"[4] It happens one step at a time.

The enemy rarely pushes us off the cliff, so to speak. We're often led down one step at a time, one compromise at a time, one wrong choice at a time. "The demonic powers not only will give us what we crave, but they will assist us in covering it over, for a little while. That's precisely the irony," says Russell Moore. He continues:

> Often you are fueled on from one temptation to the other because you haven't been caught. This gives you an illusion of a cocoon protecting you from justice. The powers, though, don't want you to get caught—not yet, not this early in the march to the slaughterhouse. They don't have a mere seventy or eighty years to live. They are ancient and patient and quite willing to wait until

---

[4] Dan Delzell, "Google Executive's Tragic Death Sends Somber Warning," *The Christian Post*, July 17, 2014, https://www.christianpost.com/news/google-executives-tragic-death-sends-somber-warning.html.

your downfall will bring with it the most catastrophic consequences—for you, for your family,
for the kingdom of God, and to the image of Christ
you carry. So they'll help you cover it all up, and
then they'll expose you—mercilessly.[5]

Praise God if your bad habits vanish once you surrender
to God, but many times it's not that easy—it's a battle. Why
God completely takes away addiction in some but allows it to
remain in others is a mystery. The words a fellow believer
spoke to me many years ago demonstrated the confusion that
many have in this area. He said, "When I was saved, God completely removed the desire for alcohol. He will remove that desire from anyone if they are truly saved." That's not always
true. Moore again hits the nail on the head:

> Sometimes we actually empower Satan by the
> way we speak of Christian conversion. We high-
> light the testimony of the ex-alcoholic who says,
> "Since I met Jesus I've never wanted another
> drink." Now that happens sometimes, and we
> should give thanks for God's power here. But this
> liberation is no more miraculous, indeed in some
> ways less so, than the testimony of the repentant
> drunk who says, "Every time I hear a clink of ice
> in a glass I tremble with desire, but God is faithful
> in keeping me sober."[6]

Change is possible. You are not beyond God's reach, but it
can be a struggle. Someone wisely said, "Where the battle

---

[5] Russell D. Moore, *Tempted and Tried* (Wheaton, IL: Crossway, 2011), 57.

[6] Moore, 72.

rages, there the loyalty of the soldier is tested." For every person God delivered completely, I can name others who still battle. Life is an *ongoing* battle. When we are on God's side, we are also on the enemy's hit list. Resistance tests our faith, draws us closer to God, and can lead to spiritual maturity.

Those who don't understand the Bible often view obedience as bondage and rules; I see it as safety and protection. I often say, "God's absolutes are guardrails through the canyons of life. They don't prevent us from enjoying life—they protect us from falling." We are to rest in God as we lovingly follow Him. It's not about rules; it's a relationship. Jesus would often ask people, "Do you want to be made well?" (John 5:6). Do you?

Although theologians are divided on the motive behind such a question, one thought is clear: we must "want" to change. Ironically, I received the following email while working on this book:

> I'm an ER nurse and I care for many people with addiction. Sadly, they love their sin and often play the victim. Most of them don't want to change, including believers. They do not want to see themselves for who they really are; their pride doesn't allow them to submit themselves to God.

As you can see, choosing to change from the inside out is the first and most important step. Even if you've relapsed many times over or completely given up hope, turn your life fully over to God today. Ask Him for the strength to overcome addiction.

Take it further: For added motivation, watch my sermon entitled "God, Change Me, and Please Hurry," on YouTube at https://youtu.be/YlmAjdMW23o or on Vimeo at https://vimeo.com/274406649.

3

Resisting Temptation—The Impossible Is Possible

In my book *Desperate for More of God*, I mentioned a long bike ride I took in the desert years ago. After I rode a great distance, I turned around and began the long journey back to my truck. I then realized that I was completely out of water. Each mile brought a new level of thirst and desperation. My thoughts were consumed with water; nothing else mattered. The calm scenery I had enjoyed minutes earlier lost its attraction. Would I make it back, or would I die in the desert?

Hope surged when I spotted my truck in the distance. Within minutes, I dropped my bike, forced the truck door open, and guzzled the remaining water. Dehydration and exhaustion quickly gave way to a refreshing sense of satisfaction. The desperate thirst I had been feeling was now satisfied. This parallels the thirst that God describes in His Word—those who thirst for Him (seek Him) with all their hearts will be satisfied.

Temptation seeks to draw us away from God. Here are a few ways to overcome temptation while seeking God:

1. You can say no. The devil can't make you do anything; he can only influence and deceive. All temptation is common to man, but "God is faithful; he will not let you be tempted beyond what you can bear. But when you are tempted, he will also provide a way out so that you can endure it" (1 Corinthians 10:13 NIV). But if you fall, God can use that brokenness to rebuild, if you surrender all to Him.

The power to say no is possible through the aid of the Holy Spirit. Endurance and perseverance are vitally important. Overcoming temptation is not easy, but it is possible—it's one hallmark of the Christian life. Persevering through pressure-filled times of temptation, while trusting in Christ to see you through, is often the most difficult part of overcoming. But be encouraged—the desire will eventually leave, and joy will follow. The theme of this book is *don't give up—look up—and ask for God's help.* Severe cravings and withdrawals are often part of the cleansing and renewing process. Every hour that goes by is one step closer to your goal.

Make prayer, worship, and the study of His Word a daily discipline, regardless of how you feel. We must reprogram our minds. God's Word is true: "Submit yourselves, then, to God. Resist the devil, and he will flee from you" (James 4:7 NIV). Resistance is not easy, but it is essential.

> IF WE FIND OURSELVES SAYING, "I TRIED THAT. IT DOESN'T WORK!" IT MAY BE BECAUSE WE TRIED OUTWARD REFORM RATHER THAN INWARD RENEWAL.

If we find ourselves saying, "I tried that. It doesn't work!" it may be because (1) we tried outward reform rather than inward renewal, (2) we gave up when it became difficult, or (3) we relied only on willpower rather than the power of the Holy Spirit. Use your failures as stepping-stones rather than excuses to continue the addiction.

22

Christians shouldn't say, "I just couldn't help myself." Scripture is clear that we have a choice. First Peter 1:14 says, "As obedient children, not conforming yourselves to the former lusts, as in your ignorance." First John 3:3 adds that "everyone who has this hope in Him purifies himself, just as He is pure." Romans 6:19 tells us to present our "[bodies] as slaves of righteousness." And 2 Peter 3:11 tells us that we ought to live holy and godly lives. These Scriptures, and many more, reveal that we can make the right decision. Matthew Henry said, "The more we follow that which is good, the faster and the further we shall flee from that which is evil."[1]

But again, be encouraged—God can use our failures and brokenness to rebuild our lives if we humble ourselves.

2. Don't plan ahead to sin (Romans 13:14). Before sin is acted on, it's conceived in the mind. For example, instead of planning to stop for a drink, a pill, or a hit after work because you "had a hard day," plan on exercising or reading. Be prepared for hard days. Don't use them as an excuse to sin but as a way to seek God more fervently. Instead of plotting how to get another thirty-day prescription of painkillers, develop a thirty-day health prioritization. Instead of scheming to look online when your spouse will be gone, prearrange God-centered activities. When we plan on sinning, we usually do. It also helps to call someone you trust (a believing spouse is often best) and have them pray with you. This simple act exposes the darkness and strengthens us via humility. When we keep sin secret, it gains strength.

---

[1] Matthew Henry, *Concise Commentary on the Whole Bible*, Bible Hub, s.v. "2 Timothy 2:22–26," accessed September 5, 2019, https://biblehub.com/commentaries/mhc/2_timothy/2.htm.

I've noticed that the enemy will build a stronghold in our lives one brick at a time, one compromise at a time. For example, many fall back into alcoholism by thinking they can have one drink after months or years of abstinence. Or they begin drinking non-alcoholic beer, which contains minimal alcohol, or fermented health drinks. The small amount of alcohol may keep the addiction alive, much like how a burner on low heat keeps meals warm. Compromise must be eradicated, not warmed; removed, not welcomed.

Side note: I've known people who didn't bring their wallet when they left the house during the first few weeks of recovery—no money, no struggle. They removed the temptation and didn't *plan* to sin. Others install location apps on their phones as a way of demonstrating transparency and accountability. These precautions aren't the answer in and of themselves, but they can help.

3. Take captive every thought (2 Corinthians 10:5). When desire comes, change the environment. That often means exchanging the friends who pull you down with new friends who will build you up. Turn to prayer, worship, and the Word rather than social media, YouTube, and television. You cannot fill your mind with the world and expect to overcome strongholds. You cannot fill your mind with darkness and expect the light of Christ to shine in your life. Strongholds are either strengthened or weakened by our thoughts. Choose wisely.

When I would get the desire to drink in the early afternoons, I had a choice: continue to dwell on it or redirect my thoughts. If I lingered upon it, I would begin to compromise. I knew Romans 13:14, "Make no provision for the flesh, to fulfill its lusts," by heart but would willingly disobey. I would plan ahead to sin. But on the flip side, if I prayed when the desire surfaced and went on a walk or studied the Bible, the desire would subside.

Victory is right around the corner as you stay focused on taking each thought captive and don't give up—which leads us to the next point.

4. Continue regardless of immediate results. The flesh (our sinful impulses) and our feelings are not friends to be trusted. A quote often attributed to Puritan author John Owen reads, "Secret lusts lie lurking in your own heart that will never give up until they are either destroyed or satisfied."[2] Paul, in Romans 8:7, tells us, "The carnal mind is enmity against God." In short, the flesh says, "Feed me so I can destroy you—destroy your health, your relationships, and your soul." C. H. Spurgeon warned his congregants, "Beware of no man more than of yourself; we carry our worst enemies within us."[3] That's why perseverance and faith in God, regardless of how we *feel*, is vitally important.

I'm not discounting the deep emotional, psychological, and physical pain associated with addiction. These pains are real and debilitating. You can't just "get over it." But I do want to remind you that God makes provision for all our needs through our relationship with Him and by our obeying His Word via perseverance, humility, and repentance.

5. It is God who makes us stand firm (2 Corinthians 1:21). Self-control is a wonderful gift from God, but it's

---

[2] John Owen, *Triumph Over Temptation: Pursuing a Life of Purity*, ed. James M. Houston (Colorado Springs, CO: Victor, 2005), 151.

[3] Charles Spurgeon, *Essential Works of Charles Spurgeon*, ed. Daniel Partner (Uhrichsville, OH: Barbour, 2009).

not the answer in and of itself. We are utterly dependent on Him: "When I am weak, then I am strong" (2 Corinthians 12:10). In 2 Corinthians 12:9, God reminds us that His grace is sufficient and His power is made perfect in weakness. God rebuilds the broken, exalts the humble, and strengthens the weak, but we must create an environment for spiritual growth. Do your part, and God will do His. Unmask the problem, install defenses, avoid whatever sparks sin, and revisit these points often. God is faithful to lead those who are willing to follow. The enemy tempts us to draw us away from God; God allows that temptation to draw us closer to Him (although He never does the tempting; see James 1).

One of the difficult challenges associated with pastoring is witnessing the tragic results of people dying spiritually because they have succumbed to temptation over a long period of time, even though incredible encouragement is just a step away: "Whoever drinks of the water that I shall give him will never thirst" (John 4:14). Although most can quote "Blessed are those who hunger and thirst for righteousness, for they shall be filled" (Matthew 5:6), many have never truly experienced it. Very few are truly hungry and thirsty for God. This thirst is an all-consuming passion that will drive addiction out of our minds and away from our hearts. If you are bound to sin, and temptation keeps taking you down, admit it to God. Humble yourself and repent. Say, "God, I am so weak in this area. Please help me. I want the 'Living Water' to overflow me with peace and purpose."

WHERE OUR MIND GOES, OUR FEET FOLLOW.

In closing this chapter, I will remind you of an important truth. Don't think about how to gratify sinful desires. Where our mind goes, our feet follow. Remove anything that causes you to sin. The man trying to kick a gambling habit shouldn't "plan" his next trip to Las Vegas. The unmarried young couple trying to stay abstinent shouldn't "plan" a night alone with wine and a movie. The addicted teenager shouldn't "plan" to meet his dealer Friday after school. The recovering addict should not "plan" a doctor's appointment to refill her prescription. The recovering alcoholic should not "plan" his summer vacation at a location that will pull him back into bondage. The recovering porn addict should not "plan" a time to go online when he will be the most vulnerable. You get the picture. This is not rocket science. Even the person fighting a food or caffeine addiction should not fill his or her pantry with enticements. "Make no provision for the flesh" is one of the best ways to cut off regret before it even starts.

Take it further: Search the word *temptation* at ShaneIdleman.com or WCFAV.org for more helpful sermons and resources.

Holiness will cost a man his sins.
He must be willing to give up
every habit and practice that is wrong
in God's sight. . . . There must be no
separate truce with any
special sin which he loves.

— *J. C. Ryle*

4

The Fully Surrendered Life

I received the following correspondence from a man who described his life before he fully surrendered to Christ:

> I had become someone I never thought I would become. I was in complete darkness . . . I would sleep in my clothes for as long as I could. I began wishing that I would die. The emotional pain was unbearable.

Experts say that thousands of churches close every year in America. And thousands of people leave the church every week, largely because church is "boring and irrelevant." Many churches are boring because the power of God has vanished from the pulpit as well as the pew. Like Samson, they do not know that the Spirit of the Lord has departed (Judges 16:20). But there is hope if we once again seek God.

The biggest breakthrough I experienced was when I surrendered my entire life to God. Full surrender leads to true peace, fulfillment, and joy. This doesn't mean you will never struggle again, but it does mean there is hope for the journey. I vividly remember a radio interview I once did. One of the callers said that he was afraid of the fully surrendered life. I replied that I was more afraid of *not* surrendering my life. What does full surrender look like? Picture a one-year-old child raising her hands to her loving parents to carry, provide for, love, and protect her. That's the image of surrender.

In today's culture, countless things entice us away from a fully surrendered life, and the enemy's schemes are designed to derail us. It is my firm belief that, second only to salvation, the fully surrendered life is the most important aspect of the Christian life. God tells us that "you will seek Me and find Me, when you search for Me with all your heart" (Jeremiah 29:13). Yet very few of us ever experience this close relationship with Him. Why? The fully surrendered life involves humility, dying to self, vibrant prayer, and heartfelt worship—things the average Christian isn't willing to do. This isn't meant to discourage you but to convict, and conviction is a wonderful gift from God used to turn the heart back to Him.

Many know 2 Chronicles 7:14: "If My people who are called by My name will humble themselves, and pray and seek My face, and turn from their wicked ways, then I will hear from heaven, and will forgive their sin and heal their land." But they often fail to apply it. God's call is not to Hollywood, to Washington, or to the media but to us. This is critical to understand for Christians, especially those caught up in any kind of addiction. In other words, "If My people turn back to Me," God says, "I will heal and restore."

To *seek* in the context of 2 Chronicles 7:14 means to "find what is missing." If Israel drifted from God, they were to return to Him by seeking Him. The same principle applies today. The Hebrew word for seek, *baqash,* has a very strong meaning. Imagine losing your child in a crowded mall. Your entire heart would be engaged. How would you spend your time? Where would your energy be concentrated? Now parallel this with seeking God.

Is It a Disease?

Let's be honest. How many of us can truly say, like Jeremiah, "His word was in my heart like a burning fire shut up in my bones; I was weary of holding it back, and I could not" (Jeremiah 20:9)? How many of us have actually experienced Jesus's words in John 7:38, "He who believes in me, as the Scripture has said, out of his heart will flow rivers of living water"? Who can say they have had the "times of refreshing" described in Acts 3:19?

Many have head knowledge, but they've never truly experienced the presence of God. Again, it's often because they have not fully surrendered their life, as illustrated in these famous lines by Wilbur Rees:

> I would like to buy $3 worth of God, please.
> Not enough to explode my soul or disturb my
> sleep, but just enough to equal a cup of warm milk
> or a snooze in the sunshine. . . . I want ecstasy, not
> transformation; I want the warmth of the womb,
> not a new birth. I want a pound of the Eternal in
> a paper sack. I would like to buy $3 worth of God,
> please. [1]

So poignant, but very true. How long will we waver? If God is God, follow Him (1 Kings 18:21).

Sadly, many believe that they have a disease that cannot be overcome. Mislabeling addiction hurts, not helps. Many

---

[1] Wilbur E. Rees, *$3.00 Worth of God* (Valley Forge, PA: Judson, 1971).

years ago, addicts were often viewed as bad people, and because of this, professionals and physicians fought to redefine the public's perceptions of addiction. Their intentions, like many today, may have been good, but calling addiction a disease is not wise because it often leads to blame-shifting.

> If it is a disease, it is the only disease without germs or virus. If it is a disease, it is the only disease that is self-inflicted. If it is a disease, it is the only disease contracted by the act of the "will." If it is a disease, it is the only disease that is bottled and sold over the counter for profit. . . . If it is a disease, it is the only disease that takes thousands of outlets in every town and city to spread it. . . . If it's a disease, it's the only disease that will cause a father to go home, grab his baby by the legs and shake him violently. If it is a disease, it's the only disease that will cause a mother to desert her children. If it's a disease, it's the only disease that will take clothes from their back and shoes from their feet and bread from their table. . . . If it is a disease, then it's the only disease that will keep one out of heaven and send that soul to hell. That sir, is not a disease; it's an addiction called sin.[2]

Please don't misunderstand. I'm aware that brain chemistry changes occur when addiction takes place. As stated earlier, we cannot just tell someone to get over it and move on without offering them a plan and giving them hope. But true freedom is found in taking responsibility, removing excuses, and asking God for help.

---

[2] Sermon excerpt from Greg Laurie.

You Have to Want To

"I've had enough! I'm filing for divorce! You will never change," yelled the once-loving spouse as the door slammed behind her. Sadly, this scenario happens all too often. Change is difficult, but we risk endless difficulties—and often, tragedies—if we don't change. Change requires self-examination, grace, responsibility, humility, discipline, and obedience, character qualities that run countercultural. We have enough books and sermons on change to fill countless libraries—our problem isn't with *how to*, it's with *want to*.

I vividly remember a men's conference where I spoke on the dangers of pornography. A man approached me afterward. With tear-filled eyes, he said, "My wife is leaving me because of porn. This conference is my last chance." After talking and praying, we isolated that his desire was being fed primarily through TV programs, including a prominent sports channel. Explicit commercials, cheerleaders, and other graphic images sparked his lust. I told him, "In addition to repentance, accountability, and transparency, remove the television and disconnect the internet for a while. Show your wife that your marriage is worth more." His response was alarming but characteristic of many today: "I can't do that! I'm a sports fanatic." Surprised and disappointed, I asked, "How badly do you want it? How badly do you want a healthy marriage and a vibrant relationship with the Lord? How badly do you want the abundant life that Christ spoke of? How badly do you want to be a godly role model for your kids? Obviously, not badly enough."

I ask the same question to you today: "How badly do you want change?" It all starts here. You must be desperate for change. It may sound simplistic, but it's true. Lies, excuses, and deception must be exchanged with honesty, responsibility, and transparency.

God may use your periods of flirting with addiction to reveal blind spots. Don't downplay the grip it has on you. If anything, play it up. A hard heart only opens the door for deeper bondage. Humbling yourself is essential. Ask yourself, "Would I continue this destructive habit if I never got caught?" If the answer is yes, then you have not humbled yourself and fully repented. Ask God for deep brokenness and dependence on Him, and ask a solid believer to pray with you. It's humiliating to tell a spouse or a close friend to pray for us because we are struggling with something, but it brings tremendous peace and exposes the sinful desires. The light will always conquer darkness. Once sin is exposed through confession and repentance, it brings light and transparency, a sense of freedom. In short, expose sin before it exposes you. Unfortunately, many people try to fight temptation on their own. Again, the door of temptation swings both ways—we can enter or exit.

Do you recall the pain of the young man in the opening paragraph of this chapter? Here is what he said after he fully surrendered his life: "I only wish that everyone could feel the love that I experienced. I'm able to forgive others and genuinely love them. I feel like I have been reborn. . . . Elusive peace has now been found."

As I said before, it's really all about Who you know. You need to be building on the solid foundation of Jesus Christ rather than the shifting sands of self-gratification and worldly wisdom. *Desperate for more of God* can be the heart cry that sets us free. He is our only hope.

Take it further:

Watch "A Spirit-Drenching Experience" on Vimeo at https://vimeo.com/272140553.

Watch these two sermons to spark revival in your heart:

"True Revival Has a Cost" can be found on YouTube at https://www.youtube.com/watch?v=zYfN3jHqek4&t=1351s

"WARNING: This Sermon Will Offend!" is available on Vimeo at https://vimeo.com/82531955

5

The Cost of Addiction

I destroy homes, tear families apart, take your children, and that's just the start.

I'm more costly than diamonds, more costly than gold, the sorrow I bring is a sight to behold.

Just try me once and I might let you go, but try me twice, and I'll own your soul.

When I possess you, you'll steal and you'll lie. You do what you have to just to get high.

You'll forget your morals and how you were raised, I'll be your conscience, I'll teach you my ways.

I take kids from parents, and parents from kids, I turn people from God, and separate from friends.

I'll take everything from you, your looks and your pride, I'll be with you always, right by your side.

I'll take and take, till you have nothing more to give. When I'm finished with you, you'll be lucky to live.

If you try me, be warned, this is no game. If given the chance, I'll drive you insane.

I'll ravish your body; I'll control your mind. I'll own you completely; your soul will be mine.

The nightmares I'll give you while lying in bed, the voices you'll hear from inside your head,

the sweats, the shakes, the visions you'll see; I want you to know, these are all gifts from me.

But then it's too late, and you'll know in your heart, that you are mine, and we shall not part.

You'll regret that you tried me, they always do, but you came to me, not I to you.

You knew this would happen. Many times you were told, but you challenged my power, and chose to be bold.

You could have said no, and just walked away. If you could live that day over now what would you say?

I'll be your master; you will be my slave, I'll even go with you, when you go to your grave.

Now that you have met me, what will you do? Will you try me or not? It's all up to you.

I can bring you more misery than words can tell. Come take my hand, let me lead you to hell.

This poem has various versions and is commonly attributed to a few different people, but regardless of the author, the points are very powerful.

Clearly, a destructive lifestyle devoid of God can be hell on earth. Even seemingly innocent addictions can wreak havoc on our health and family. They affect attitudes in a very negative way. First Peter 2:11 urges us to "abstain from fleshly lusts which wage war against the soul." But I don't want to leave you with condemnation—conviction, yes, but condemnation, no.

When I challenge people in this area, I often ask them, "Are you genuinely sorry and repentant, or are you just sorry that your reputation and life are on the verge of being ruined?" The difference between sorrow and repentance is vital because many confuse the two. It's possible to be sorry about the "consequences" of addiction but not be truly repentant. This is why many return to their former state. They rationalize and make excuses for addiction. By excusing actions, we deny responsibility. Ironically, as I'm writing this chapter, a friend of mine keeps blaming his alcoholism on his spouse, and he will die soon if he continues down this very destructive path. This is why pride is so dangerous.

A penitent person turns from sin. Anger, for example, subsides, not remains. Those who are repentant accept full responsibility for their actions without blame, resentment, or bitterness. When repentance is genuine, we want to be reconciled with those we've injured. We seek forgiveness without conditions and stipulations. We take full, not partial, responsibility for our actions. We don't blame "this and that"; there can be no "buts" when repentance is genuine. "I am sorry. I was wrong. Please forgive me," are often (although not always) healing words and signs of repentance. If this is not occurring, repentance has not taken place.

Again, I'm not minimizing the deep pain, emotional toll, and spiritual struggle that addiction brings, but I do want to remind you that God makes provision for all our needs—spiritually, mentally, emotionally, and physically. As stated earlier, we must surrender to Him. Many are already surrendered but to the wrong thing.

Here is a nugget of hope: overcoming addiction has a great deal to do with *falling forward*. This is not a license to sin, but it is an encouragement to those who keep falling. Get back up! God uses our failures to remind us of our need for Him. Once we look to Him for guidance, strongholds begin to lose their power. The allurement of sin begins to weaken its grip. Some strongholds don't immediately crumble; they come down one brick at a time. Get out the fifteen-pound sledgehammer and go to work! Pray, fast, apply the Word, worship and trust in God—this is how we fight our battles.

> **SOME STRONGHOLDS DON'T IMMEDIATELY CRUMBLE; THEY COME DOWN ONE BRICK AT A TIME.**

Years ago, seemingly out of nowhere, a fiery dart was shot at me. An intense desire to drink alcohol came over me. I felt helpless—almost as if I were a puppet in the hands of a cruel master. But by God's grace, I called on Him and began to worship Him. As soon as I made that decision, the cravings began to diminish. They didn't disappear right away, but the grip loosened (one brick at a time). This is the "way of escape" we talked about earlier. The idol of addiction needs to be crushed, not coddled.

I vividly remember one young woman who was addicted to painkillers. Her use eventually led to harder drugs that ultimately led to a deadly overdose that sent shock waves through our congregation. As I spoke at the memorial service, I saw hundreds of broken lives and deep bondage (many attendees were even high). Though their pain, visible on their faces, was real, I was able to offer hope and encouragement.

I also recall another time when a young man lost visitation rights to see his young daughter. His use of oxycodone had finally taken its toll. It promised pleasure but brought regret and imprisonment. I've counseled many who've admitted that alcohol or substance abuse ruined their marriage and drove their children further away from God.

God can pull you out of the deepest pit and the lowest point of despair as well. The greater the pain, the more we appreciate our Redeemer. Remember again Luke 7:47: those who have been forgiven much, love much. Even if you're at your absolute lowest point, there is hope. God can pull you out of the pit.

Addiction is Satan's tool to kill, steal, and destroy. The enemy doesn't show a person the pain, anguish, and years of regret that addiction brings; rather, he deceives with temporary enjoyment. Then they fall back into shame and depression, and the cycle of bondage often continues.

We also must be very careful when it comes to pain management. Countless people became addicted to drugs as a result of medicating their pain. I estimate that nearly 30 percent of the people I pray with about addiction got hooked this way.

My advice is to use short-term and minimal dosages if you must go that route.

A wise man once said, "When faced with temptation, play the whole tape in your mind." In other words, don't focus on the temporary pleasure; look at where it will lead. Private sin will eventually become public disgrace. A commentary on Genesis brings this point home:

> Esau acted on impulse, satisfying his immediate desires without pausing to consider the long-range consequences of what he was about to do. ... When we see something we want, our first impulse is to get it. ... We might feel such great pressure in one area that nothing else seems to matter and we lose our perspective. Getting through that short, pressure-filled moment is often the most difficult part of overcoming a temptation.[1]

The Cost of Addiction

Addiction hinders our relationship with God. I've never met a person who felt close to God while continuing in an addiction. Acts 3:19 says that repentance leads to times of refreshing with the Lord. Take that step today and experience refreshment and joy again.

A WISE MAN ONCE SAID, "WHEN FACED WITH TEMPTATION, PLAY THE WHOLE TAPE IN YOUR MIND."

Addiction turns into idolatry. The opposite of worship is idolatry. Romans 1:25 (NIV)

---

[1] *NIV Study Bible* notes on Genesis 25:32–33 (Grand Rapids: Zondervan, 1991).

speaks of idolaters who "exchanged the truth about God for a lie" by worshiping and serving created things rather than the Creator.

Addiction damages our relationship with our spouse, children, family, and friends. We feed our addiction versus investing time with those we love. How many boys want their father to play catch? How many girls want daddy time? Kids need our attention. We are competing with a society that is always busy but rarely doing anything noteworthy. This applies to smartphones and social media as well; they are time zappers. Moreover, ministry is stifled and spiritual growth minimized when addiction prevails.

Addiction fuels irritability and anger. We snap more easily when under pressure, which can also lead to rude and manipulative behavior. Addiction controls, influences, and provokes anger. Alcohol often fuels angry temper tantrums and explosive outbursts. Addiction to caffeine often does the same; it's a powerful stimulant that feeds anger, irritability, and a quick temper (i.e., hotheadedness).

The *Diagnostic and Statistical Manual of Mental Disorders* lists caffeine-related disorders such as caffeine intoxication, caffeine-induced anxiety disorder, and caffeine-induced sleep disorder.[2] All can lead to angry outbursts and extreme irritability. Again, don't rationalize and make excuses for addiction. By excusing actions, we deny responsibility. Take responsibility and make the needed changes.

---

[2] American Psychiatric Association, *Diagnostic and Statistical Manual of Mental Disorders (DSM-IV)* (Arlington, VA: American Psychiatric Association, 2000), 232.

Addiction leads to financial difficulty. Overspending and poor choices feed the addiction and vice versa. It's difficult to maintain employment when one is addicted, and even those who remain employed can never seem to get it together.

Addiction hinders God's blessings. God will not fully bless those living in disobedience. When sin runs its course, it often hurts careers, ministries, health, and everything that God has blessed us with.

At the heart of addiction is idolatry; therefore, we need heart surgery to remove the idol that has taken up residency. Psychologists are familiar with the term *cognitive dissonance*, which defines the battle inside a person who believes one way yet acts another. But God calls addiction *sin* and uses conviction to bring us in line with His truth. Although many wonderful, godly counselors anchor their counsel in the Word of God, scores of others offer advice contrary to Scripture. For example:

Psychology says	Scripture says
The heart is good.	The heart is deceitful.
You just need to unlock your inner strength.	Willpower is not enough.
Don't lay a guilt trip on the addict.	Conviction is good.
It's not really your fault.	Confess your sins and repent.
Therapy is the answer.	Christ is the answer.

Saying, "Don't lay a guilt trip on me," might make you feel better, but it's not biblical, and it will not help. The guilt, fear, and conviction we can feel are used by God to draw us to repentance and are wholly appropriate. Professional counselors, for example, can be a wonderful resource if they get to the root of the problem and don't write off shame and guilt. When we hurt, we should turn to God, not try to excuse our behavior.

If those who offer counsel minimize conviction, they may actually enable the person and hinder the work that God may be doing in their heart. I'm not suggesting we refrain from comforting people, but comfort should not replace conviction. As stated at the beginning of this book, the first step toward freedom is recognizing our need for a Savior and turning to Him. Conviction often points us in His direction. Don't allow guilt and shame to continue ruining your life. Proverbs 13:15 (KJV) states that "the way of the transgressors is hard," but 1 John 1:9 offers us hope, "If we confess our sins, He is faithful and just to forgive us our sins and to cleanse us from all unrighteousness."

Breaking Free

Now that we have covered the cost of addiction, here are a few takeaways to help you start taking steps in the right direction. Some of this is a recap of what's been discussed thus far.

Repentance must take place. I realize I'm using the word *repentance* a lot, but I'd rather talk too much about it than too little. Sadly, many are confused about repentance, and most pulpits avoid the word altogether. Some even say that repentance is self-improvement or a call to fulfill our natural potential. When we repent, we do improve and our God-given potential becomes more apparent, but repentance is not about self-improvement—it's about renouncing sin and turning from it.

Repentance is a change of mind that leads to a change in action. Brokenness, genuine sorrow over sin, and humility are marks of sincere repentance. Lasting hope and joy are also by-products of a right relationship with God, beginning with repentance. When confronted, many will say they are sorry, but deep down they want to enjoy sin again. J. C. Ryle hits the nail head on: "Holiness will cost a man his sins. He must be willing to give up every habit and practice which is wrong in God's sight. . . . There must be no separate truce with any special sin which he loves."[3] There is always a link between genuine change and sincere repentance.

> **HOLINESS WILL COST A MAN HIS SINS.**
> —J. C. RYLE

Ask God for help. We must seek to identify the middle ground between our responsibility and God's role in changing us. If the pendulum swings too much in the grace direction, obedience will suffer. Some may not agree with this statement, but the Bible is filled with passages dealing with obedience. For example, James 1:22 says, "But be doers of the word, and not hearers only, deceiving yourselves." Obedience is a hallmark of the faith, as seen in 1 John 2:3–4: "Now by this we know that we know Him, if we keep His commandments. He who says, 'I know [Christ],' and does not keep His commandments, is a liar, and the truth is not in him." The word *keep*

---

3 J. C. Ryle, *Holiness* (Lafayette, IN: Sovereign Grace, 2001), 44.

here means "to keep watchful care of." In the same way that a ship's captain is committed to keep his course to reach his destination, the sincerity of our commitment to Christ can be measured by how well we follow the scriptural course via obedience. Sanctification is God's job, but obedience is ours.

On the other hand, if the pendulum swings too much in the obedience direction, one may become a rule-following legalist who never experiences God's wonderful grace. Legalism can be defined as a self-righteous attitude that rates spirituality by how well a person follows rules—Christ plus something equals morality. Legalism prevents change because it hardens the heart. The legalist often justifies their behavior because "they are right"—at least in their own eyes.

> **SANCTIFICATION IS GOD'S JOB, BUT OBEDIENCE IS OURS.**

Be careful because pride is at the root of all sin. Proud people often don't change until they are broken and humbled. Brokenness, humility, and full surrender provide fertile ground for change. We have responsibilities, yet we are totally dependent on God. We must do our part, but we can't do His. Again, it is God who makes us stand firm in Christ (2 Corinthians 1:21). Seek Him.

Avoid excuses and the victim mentality. When we fail to take responsibility for our actions, the endless cycle of blame, anger, and unforgiveness often continues. Those enslaved by blame and unforgiveness are truly imprisoned, and the walls they build to protect themselves may eventually imprison them. These destructive forces prohibit change. By excusing our actions, we deny responsibility. Those who continue with harmful addictions, for example, often excuse their actions and even justify them. Don't blame your parents, your culture or race, your spouse, or the government. Take responsibility, even if it hurts.

Never underestimate the seriousness of sin. Be crystal clear on this issue: sin destroys. "Little" sins or vices that we enjoy eventually grow and become strong influences. Addiction has a life cycle—it either grows or withers depending on whether we feed or starve it. James 1:14–15 illustrates this destructive course: "But each one is tempted when he is drawn away by his own desires and enticed. Then, when desire has conceived, it gives birth to sin; and sin, when it is full-grown, brings forth death." Don't blame the devil. We are led away by our own desires; he simply presents the bait.

Jesus came to give life. Are you experiencing the abundant life that Christ spoke of? There is a negative cost to addiction, but the cost of following Christ brings tremendous hope and peace—a huge positive. We all pay a price for following someone or something. Make the choice to follow Christ today despite the cost. Take time now to read Luke 14:25–34 about truly counting the cost.

> THE AMOUNT OF DEMONIC INFLUENCE THAT COMES INTO OUR LIVES OFTEN DEPENDS ON HOW FAR WE HAVE OPENED THE DOOR.

A Quick Word about Demonic Activity

We can't rule out the possibility of a spiritual attack. Throughout the New Testament, demonic activity caused mental anguish. When a person takes powerful drugs, that may only increase the problem and could even open the door to further demonic activity. *Pharmakeía* (from where we get our word *pharmacy*) means to administer drugs. In the Bible, it was often tied to the practice of magic and sorcery. But before seeking to deal with a spirit of division, humble yourself. Before blaming a spirit of lust, flee from it. You don't have to cast out a spirit of drunkenness—you can abstain.

I'm not minimizing demonic activity. In some cases, a person may need deliverance—I have seen my share—but the amount of demonic influence that comes into our lives often depends on how far we have opened the door. It's no surprise that the friend caught in alcoholism I mentioned earlier also enjoys dark, destructive gothic music. He feeds the demons he is trying to run from. How about you? Are you feeding what you should be fleeing? Empowering what you should be quenching?

> SOMETIMES STRONGHOLDS MUST BE PULLED DOWN ONE BRICK AT A TIME.

How do you know if an attack is demonic? Take it to God in prayer, and fast. Read Appendix 2 and see if the five points listed are playing a role. Ask for wisdom and deliverance if necessary. Have you opened any obvious doors such as messing around with palm reading, tarot cards, Ouija boards, or other occultic things? What about alcohol and drugs? Is there a family history of occult practices? Have those strong in the faith pray for you regularly. Remember, some strongholds must be pulled down one brick at a time. Saturate your mind in the Word, and pray and worship throughout the day.

6

The Power of the
Renewed Mind

Desensitization can be well illustrated through a story I heard years ago. Eskimos in the barren North often kill wolves by taking a razor-sharp knife and dipping it in blood. They allow the blood to freeze to the blade. Then they bury the handle of the knife in the snow with the blade exposed. As the wolf begins to lick the blade, his tongue becomes numb and desensitized due to the cold. As he continues, his tongue begins to bleed, and he licks even faster—unaware that he is consuming his own blood and slowly killing himself.

Soon the Eskimos return and bring the dead animal home. In the same way, the enemy numbs us through compromise by what we allow into our minds. Within time, we, like the wolves, don't see that we are dying—dying spiritually.

The enemy desensitizes us until we are numb to the things of God and our conviction fades. Why do so many people enjoy movies and programs that glorify illicit sex, witchcraft, the occult, extreme violence, vampires, and the like? Incredibly, what God calls an abomination is today's entertainment. We have no time for prayer and devotion to God but plenty of time for entertainment. Do you see the disconnect?

Is it a coincidence that many who are trapped in addiction enjoy ungodly music and movies? I think not. Entertainment indeed plays a role in how we think and what we think about. As much as I loved country music back in the day, it kept me bound to alcohol by reinforcing whiskey, women, and woe. Yes, I know there are some good country songs, as well as in other genres, but we must be discerning about what we listen to. For example, Michael W. Smith's worship song "Surrounded (Fight My Battles)" is way more encouraging to me than the George Jones hit "He Stopped Loving Her Today," for obvious reasons.

> **THE QUESTION TO ASK IS, WILL IT BUILD ME UP SPIRITUALLY OR PULL ME DOWN?**

We rationalize watching and listening to questionable material because, in most cases, we enjoy it. We have become desensitized, and our consciences have been seared. Excuses are often packaged in phrases such as "I have liberty to watch this" or "It's no big deal; everyone is doing it" or, my personal favorite, "I need to watch these things so I can relate to the culture." But we must remember that liberty has limits. The questions to ask are, *Will it build me up spiritually or pull me down? Will it fuel my addiction or quench it?*

A Christian once told me, "I don't worry about what I watch or listen to as long as my heart is right." Sadly, this comment came from a youth pastor. It's an indication of how far we have drifted. To suggest that entertainment is neutral simply reflects a lack of spiritual discernment. Some allegories of good and evil can carry a noble message; however, when evil is portrayed as good or we've become obsessed with watching them, we've crossed the line.

There are gray areas, of course, but illicit sex, enchantments, witchcraft, familiar spirits, wizards, and extreme violence are not gray areas, even if portrayed as good. Darkness should not entertain the church. A different influence—namely, the Holy Spirit—should guide us. What we watch and listen to affects the heart; it's impossible to separate the two. If you truly want to overcome strongholds, you'll need to reprogram your mind. For starters, spend time this week reading and meditating on Romans 12 and Philippians 4.

This generation greatly suffers from hopelessness and depression. Suicide is an epidemic among teens and young adults. Surely, one must wonder if there is a correlation. Do we really think that ungodly entertainment is not going to affect us or our children? Do we genuinely believe these are simply fun, entertaining shows with no spiritual ramifications? The time to renew our minds has never been greater.

Ephesians 6:12 (NIV) reminds us that "our struggle is not against flesh and blood, but against the rulers, against the authorities, against the powers of this dark world and against the spiritual forces of evil in the heavenly realms." For this reason, Psalm 101:3 warns us not to put anything wicked before our eyes, and 1 Timothy 4:12 exhorts us to be examples of purity and decency. Philippians 4:8 says to fix our thoughts on what is true and honorable and right and to think about things that are pure, lovely, admirable, and worthy of praise.

Everyone who names the name of Christ must depart from anything that goes against His standard of holiness if they truly desire spiritual health. Freedom cannot come from a polluted mind. Galatians 6:7 (ESV) gives us a stark reminder: "Do not be deceived. God is not mocked, for whatever one sows, that will he also reap."

Sadly, most people don't turn their life over to God when things are going well. Repentance is often sparked by catastrophic failure. We often need a wakeup call before we wake up. God crushes our pride to open our ears, but you don't have to wait until you hit rock bottom. God promises deliverance if we turn to Him, but again, this doesn't always happen overnight. Breaking strongholds and reprogramming our thinking are battles that can take time. For instance, I know Christians who haven't had a drop of alcohol in years but still struggle when someone drinks a beer or a glass of wine in their presence. The battle is truly fought in the mind.

Humility recognizes that we are fallible human beings who have sinned against God. His Word is a lifeline to our soul, an anchor for our lives, not something to be debated, altered, or misrepresented. We don't change truth—truth changes us.

In closing this chapter, let's summarize three key points to renewing the mind:

- **Be aware of "opportune times."** Luke 4:13 (NIV) says, "And when the devil had ended every temptation, he departed from him until an opportune time." In battle, the enemy attacks at opportune times. "Opportune times" in the Greek language denotes a favorable wind blowing a ship toward its destination. The world entices us through cravings for physical pleasure, through covetousness, and through pride in our achievements and possessions. These are the three areas where the enemy will concentrate his focus. Be aware of these "opportune times."

- **The source of our strength comes from the food that we choose.** What we feed grows, and what grows becomes the strong, dominating force within our lives. Our thoughts become words, our words become actions, our actions become habits. Who or what is shaping your thoughts? A daily diet of violence, lust, anger, and depression will fuel those very things in your life. The old saying, "The devil made me do it," is false. Again, the devil doesn't *make* us do anything; he simply presents the bait. James 1:14–15 says that each of us is tempted when we are drawn away by our own evil desires. Then, after the desire has been acted out, it gives birth to sin; and sin, when it is full-grown, leads to death (i.e., feed me so I can destroy you).

- **Be encouraged.** When you truly seek God's help, you can overcome temptation instead of allowing temptation to overcome you. The key is to pray for strength and wisdom, to be mindful of the warfare and the weapons of warfare (see Ephesians 6), then choose accordingly. This falls in line with Romans 12:2 instructing us to renew our minds. When we yield to temptation, we walk willingly into the enemy's camp and quench and grieve the Spirit within us. An immediate full turn in the opposite direction at the first sign of temptation will encourage victory.

The Power of Prayer

The importance of time alone with God cannot be stressed enough. It is invaluable. Renewal begins and ends with prayer.

To renew means to reestablish something after it has been interrupted or damaged. Life can easily interrupt fellowship with God, but we are renewed through prayer and time alone with Him. Mighty fillings of the Spirit often occur after extended times of prayer.

IT'S HARD TO FALL WHEN YOU'RE ALWAYS ON YOUR KNEES.

I will never forget New Year's Eve of 2011. I spent some time alone in a cabin to slow down, reflect, pray, and renew my mind. During this private time of renewal, I was reminded that the overall spiritual condition of Westside Christian Fellowship will be a reflection of my prayer life. E. M. Bounds believed that without prayer in the pulpit,

> the church becomes a graveyard, not an embattled army. Praise and prayer are stifled; worship is dead. The preacher and the preaching have helped sin, not holiness. . . . Preaching that kills is prayerless preaching. Without prayer, the preacher creates death and not life.[1]

You may ask, "What does this have to do with me? I'm not a pastor." Everything! Your overall spiritual health is a direct reflection of your prayer life. Little prayer, little health. Strongholds are broken through prayer. It's hard to fall when you're always on your knees.

Moses spent time in the backside of the desert before leading Israel out of bondage. Elijah heard the still, small voice of God while alone in a cave. Jacob wrestled with God in the stillness of the night, and his name was changed to Israel.

---

[1] E. M. Bounds, *Pastor and Prayer: Why and How Pastors Ought to Pray* (Abbotsford, WI: Aneko, 2018), 18.

John the Baptist lived alone in constant prayer with God. Jesus often retreated to isolated places for extended times of prayer. How, then, are we going to overcome in these dire times if we do not cultivate a strong prayer life? The depth of our relationship with God is in direct proportion to the depth of our prayer life. Begin a life of prayer today. It's been said that men will live better if they pray better. Conversely, we pray better when we live better. It's all connected.

Take it further:

Two helpful sermons on prayer at YouTube:

- "Preparing the Heart to Pray": https://youtu.be/ef8H4WyWXdI
- "Teach Us to Pray": https://youtu.be/_MKP0XB-O2k

You can also search the word *prayer* at WCFAV.org and ShaneIdleman.com.

7

Overcoming Regret: Hope for the Prodigal

Many of us look back on our lives and regret the choices we have made. We didn't see it coming. We often overlook the awful consequences of sin because we're enticed by the temporary pleasure of it.

In life, we experience either the pain of discipline or the pain of regret. There are countless examples: a young parent loses visitation rights because of an addiction to pain pills, or a family is destroyed because of drug or alcohol abuse. Situations vary, but the outcome doesn't.

Regret often leads us back into bondage, and the vicious cycle continues. But we can find tremendous hope if we turn to God and encounter the pain of discipline over the pain of regret. The pain of discipline produces joy; the pain of regret produces anguish. The pain of discipline produces peace; the pain of regret produces fear. The pain of discipline produces assurance; the pain of regret produces confusion.

Psalm 107:10 opens with a stark portrayal of bondage: "Those who sat in darkness and in the shadow of death, bound in affliction and irons." Have you ever been there? Those held captive by sin can no doubt relate. Darkness and depression overshadow everything.

The wisdom in this psalm continues to expose the root of bondage: "Because they rebelled against the words of God, and despised the counsel of the Most High, therefore He brought down their heart with labor; they fell down, and there was none to help" (vv. 11–12). The imagery conveys people stumbling through life or locked in a prison where no one can come to their aid. Their hearts are heavy as the result of despising God and rejecting His truth. The only one who can truly help is the One who created us. We must cry out to the Lord in our trouble, and He will save us out of our distress (v. 13). That promise will not fail. He will bring us "out of darkness and the shadow of death," and He will "[break our] chains in pieces" (v. 14).

What a wonderful God we serve. He warns us about wandering from Him, but when we do wander and experience regret, He invites us back. But we must come with a broken and contrite heart. We must cry out to Him: "Oh, that men would give thanks to the LORD for His goodness, and for His wonderful works to the children of men! For He has broken the gates of bronze, and cut the bars of iron in two" (vv. 15–16).

Bronze and iron are very strong materials. God can break any bondage if we turn everything over to Him. Your first and most profound choice is to say no, then let God handle the rest. There may be withdrawals, consequences, and pain as we heal, but the pain of discipline is temporary, while the pain of regret lingers. Jesus often spoke out against those who enjoyed wallowing in sin, yet His love and mercy reach out to everyone who regrets their sin and hates their condition. Do you enjoy sin, or do you cry out for help? That makes all the difference.

Be encouraged, because regret can redirect a person back to God. Psalm 51:17 (NIV) says, "My sacrifice, O God, is a broken spirit; a broken and contrite heart you, God, will not despise." Regret, when used as a stepping-stone rather than a stumbling block, can rebuild marriages, families, and lives. Don't let it continue to drive you down; let it build you up.

Regret, pain, depression, fear, and anxiety are often the result of wandering from God, much like a ship that has drifted off course. Once the correct course is set, however, hope, peace, and joy return. God will bring you "out of darkness and the shadow of death" and break your "chains in pieces" (Ps. 107:14). You may be in your fifth recovery home, on your third marriage, or living in your twilight years with a past full of regret, but God can rebuild and restore.

YOU MAY BE IN YOUR FIFTH RECOVERY HOME, ON YOUR THIRD MARRIAGE, OR LIVING IN YOUR TWILIGHT YEARS WITH A PAST FULL OF REGRET, BUT GOD CAN REBUILD AND RESTORE.

Don't let discouragement and failure define you or stand in your way. I could write an entire book on my failures, but instead I try to follow the apostle Paul's advice, and I encourage you to do the same: "Forgetting those things which are behind and reaching forward to those things which are ahead" (Philippians 3:13). Forget your past mistakes but remember the lessons learned because of them. Overcome the pain of regret by allowing God to rebuild your life.

Principles to Overcome Regret

> RATHER THAN ALLOW REGRET TO KNOCK YOU OFF COURSE, USE IT TO HELP YOU STAY THE COURSE.

1. It's only over when God says it's over. Regret paralyzes progress because we feel we've done too much damage. We think, *God can't use me now.* But God always uses people who have failed if they realign their heart with His.

2. A delay is not a denial. God often prepares us so we can handle the weight of what He has called us to do. Figuratively speaking, you don't see a young apple tree bear abundant fruit; the tree would collapse under the weight. Likewise, we have growing to do. Personality issues, attitudes, and certain habits need to be adjusted. There is a saying in the construction business that "the deeper the foundation, the stronger the structure." The depth of our spiritual foundation also determines how much we can carry. Don't be frustrated; God may be building and strengthening your foundation and aligning your will with His. Rather than allow regret to knock you off course, use it to help you stay the course.

3. God's will is not easy. I once believed that life was easy in the center of God's will, and if it wasn't easy, I was out of His will. This isn't necessarily true. We should have peace in the center of God's will but not freedom from difficult circumstances. At times, we may fight bouts of anxiety, depression, and fear. Many biblical heroes fought hardship and anxiety while being in the center of God's will.

How can we determine if a challenge is the result of being in God's will or because of disobedience? First, ask yourself if your motives are honest and if there is any sin that you're harboring. Second, focus on obeying God's Word and the convictions of the Holy Spirit. Third, seek biblical counsel and use wisdom. God will direct you one way or the other.

Again, try to see challenges as opportunities for growth. Being in the center of God's will does not prevent challenges; it sometimes creates them. In Matthew 7:24–27, Jesus told the story of a wise man who built his house on solid rock (God's Word) rather than on shifting sand (man's philosophy). As a result, his house withstood the storm. On the contrary, the foolish man who built his house on sand lost everything. Notice that both men encountered the storm—adversity comes to all of us. In my life, I've seen storms come right before God opened a huge door, and they tested our faith as a family. Expect the storms, but know that you can weather them successfully as you look to God's Word for the answers and stay the course.

4. God is not on our timetable. God gives us godly desires that line up with His will. Timing is everything. It's been said that a gift from God given too soon can cause much harm. For this very reason, I thank God often for giving me kids later in life and not during my twenties. Much like an enormous jigsaw puzzle, God's will has many pieces that must come together before we see the picture. In retrospect, I see that God used my regret to reposition me. They were not *wasted* years but *waiting* years. I could go into a long pity party about how many years I squandered due to alcohol use, or I can thank God for delivering me and using me.

5. Never forget that it is God who helps us stand firm (2 Corinthians 12:9). God is faithful to lead those who are willing to follow. Are you willing to follow?

8

Pushing through Withdrawals

> I was doing fine for a few weeks, then all of a sudden, I was hit with tremendous anxiety. I tried to push back, but I eventually caved in and purchased alcohol to take the edge off. It worked temporarily, but it also caused a relapse, a relapse I'm still battling through.
>
> — Anonymous

Most people relapse when withdrawals knock at the door and they answer it. For this reason, this chapter is more important than many realize. To be forewarned is to be forearmed.

When I severely curtailed caffeine use, I experienced panic attacks unlike anything I had felt before. It was a nightmare, but I was prepared. I knew what was happening—my body was going through withdrawals.

In other words, most return to addiction because they are not prepared for what the body is about to go through. The effects of withdrawal seem unbearable, so many people go back to their drug of comfort, and the cycle of addiction is repeated . . . again . . . and again . . . and again.

The enemy uses opportune times, like withdrawals, to draw us back into bondage. The acronym HALT has been used by many organizations to highlight these times. Relapse often happens when people are **hungry**, **angry**, **lonely**, or **tired**.

With that said, I have also seen God completely deliver people from drugs and alcohol without any withdrawals. In short: *pray for heaven but expect hell.* That is, trust in God and pray for complete healing or minimal suffering, but if He takes you through the pain of withdrawals, He will be your anchor. Although I would never want to go through the torment of withdrawals from caffeine or alcohol, the brokenness, humility, and full surrender to God that happens can be priceless.

Let me state up front that it's a good idea to seek professional help when detoxing, especially if you've been abusing strong drugs for a while. Medical professionals and those skilled in rehabilitation can monitor progress, offer encouragement, and help with nutrition. In some cases, tapering off will work better, and professionals can walk you through the process. But tapering has pitfalls as well. In most cases, it's nearly impossible for an alcoholic to decrease their dosage until they are dry. Often, the reverse happens—they stay hooked.

When we take the first hit, pill, or drink, we lose the ability to say no, then the substance takes over. Again, those who have been using for a long time should consider supervised care. Xanax, for example, has significant withdrawals that may occur if a person goes cold turkey. The panic attacks and anxiety may be worse than before the person started taking the drug. Please understand that my goal is not to scare; it is to prepare. Enduring the withdrawals is better than continuing the addiction.

There are two schools of thought in the Christian community. One says that everything is spiritual and you don't need to balance out brain chemistry with medication, and if you do, you're in sin. The other school of thought, which can be just as dangerous, says that we need to medicate everything and everyone. (Be sure to read the appendix for more information on mental health.)

In my opinion, many problems are due to lifestyle choices, and therefore, we need to start there. Reaching for a pill as soon as we feel anxious is rarely the best solution. Years ago, when I was going through anxiety attacks as the result of withdrawals, my physician recommended Xanax, but medication only prolonged the problem. I only took them for a day or two. I had to ride it out. I needed to eat the right foods and take care of my body again. Although every situation is different, too many people run to a pill, a drink, or comfort food instead of running to God, or they use medication instead of fueling the body with what it needs.

First and foremost, we need to seek God through prayer and time in His Word. We need to ask Him for wisdom. Often, medication should be the last resort, not the first, and definitely not long-term whenever possible. For example, the alcoholic may start to experience anxiety a month after quitting. After a visit to the doctor, he is prescribed Xanax. Months go by, and the person is now addicted to Xanax and must start worrying about the withdrawals that may follow. It becomes a vicious cycle of detox-withdraw-start again.

It also saddens me when users and alcoholics exchange those addictions for caffeine or nicotine. They stop drinking alcohol, but now they are addicted to massive amounts of coffee, not realizing that caffeine is a powerful drug as well. Although they gave up one drug, the root problem of addiction most likely was not addressed. Granted, I'd rather have a caffeine problem than an alcohol problem, but an addiction is still in control.

Unfortunately, I cannot offer a one-size-fits-all approach to quitting certain drugs, but I do know that seeking God must be the first step. He can lessen the load and lighten the burden. He can give wisdom and direction. I also believe in consuming foods and supplements that bring life to the body. Yes, medical supervision is important in many cases depending on severity, but nobody knows our body better than the Creator. Seek Him. (For eBook readers, here is a teaching I put together to help in this area as well on health, which we'll discuss in the next chapter.[1])

Two Phases of Withdrawal

Many people are surprised to learn there are two types of withdrawals. The withdrawals that start soon after the substance is stopped are very difficult and can manifest themselves via anxiety, heart palpitations, confusion, depression, emotional mood swings, sleep disturbance, and an array of other symptoms. Time will not allow me to list all the addictions or withdrawals that accompany them, but there is plenty of good information available through reputable recovery websites.

The second stage of withdrawal is what catches people off guard. It's called Post-Acute Withdrawal Syndrome (PAWS).

---

[1] See "Get Back on Track (Health Seminar)," January 10, 2019, https://www.youtube.com/watch?v=MKD1tmB9jl8&t=4563s.

Everything can be good for a few weeks, even a few months, then suddenly a person can be gripped with fear, anxiety, and depression. In other words, the ghost that haunts returns. *Promises Behavioral Health* spells it out plainly:

> In the early days of PAWS, emotional and psychological turmoil is the norm, as the ups and downs come and go so quickly that recovering addicts will feel like their lives are careening out of control. Recovering addicts will experience alternating periods of dysfunction and near-normality throughout the post-acute stage, with the only change being that as time passes the duration of the good times will begin to increase. This is the result of the brain slowly re-organizing and re-balancing itself, and even though the negative effects associated with PAWS will remain a part of the equation for quite some time, addicts should take heart in knowing that eventually those comforting feelings of normalcy and stability will transition into a full-time state of being.

> The symptoms of PAWS are the equivalent of a ghost that haunts the soul of the recovering addict, reminding him or her over and over again of the damage they did to themselves by abusing chemical intoxicants for so long. Thankfully, over time the relentless voices of those persistent spirits will begin to fade away, until there is nothing left of them but a barely audible whisper. But if they expect to reach that final destination of sobriety, the suffering associated with PAWS is a

toll that all passengers who have taken the ride of substance abuse will have to pay.[2]

As a pastor, I have a different view than many do of the secular websites. In addition to preparing people for PAWS that may result, I would also encourage the person to seek God with all their heart and allow Him to restore and rebuild. He may heal them early, or they may go through PAWS.

Forgetting our past (but not the lessons learned) is a mental discipline. Where the mind goes, the feet follow. Philippians 4:8–9 adds, "Finally, brethren, whatever things are true, whatever things are noble, whatever things are just, whatever things are pure, whatever things are lovely, whatever things are of good report, if there is any virtue and if there is anything praiseworthy—meditate on these things."

Few are experiencing peace because their minds are set on the things of the world rather than the things of God. Life is never fulfilling until you change your perspective. Those with a deep sense of emptiness and feelings of inadequacy are not taking their "thoughts" captive according to Philippians 4. I have great compassion for those going through difficulty. I've been there. But dwelling on negativity fuels depression and anxiety and quenches and grieves the Holy Spirit. The best way to get through PAWS is with God's help.

---

[2] "A Primer on Post-Acute Withdrawal Syndrome," Promises Behavioral Health, March 2, 2013, https://www.promisesbehavioralhealth.com/addiction-recovery-blog/addiction-recovery/a-primer-on-post-acute-withdrawal-syndrome. Please understand that neither the author nor the publisher endorses all the references in this website.

Promises Behavioral Health is again helpful here:

> Be patient. You can't hurry recovery. . . . If you try to rush your recovery, or resent post-acute withdrawal, or try to bulldoze your way through, you'll become exhausted. And when you're exhausted, you'll think of using to escape. Post-acute withdrawal symptoms are a sign that your brain is recovering. They are the result of your brain chemistry gradually going back to normal.[3]

Taking care of our bodies through healthy eating, supplementation, and exercise is also a major step in recovery, which brings us to the next chapter.

---

[3] "A Primer on Post-Acute Withdrawal Syndrome."

9

The Gift of Health

I'm deeply saddened by the number of people who neglect health as if it doesn't matter to God. Life is a gift; our body is the only place we have to live. This is why this chapter is so important. Although we've discussed the health of our spirit and soul, little has been said about our physical health. Therefore, it's time to shift gears.

As I was writing this book, I was also completing *Feasting and Fasting: What Works, What Doesn't, and Why*. The following pages contain some of those excerpts. For those interested in taking better care of their body, I would encourage you to read *Feasting and Fasting* as well as *What Works When Diets Don't*.[1]

I often see a parallel between physical and spiritual health. Too many Christians are strung out on caffeine, nicotine, alcohol, pain meds, and poor eating habits. Not only are they are shipwrecking this wonderful gift God has given us but they have no passion for God. They wonder why anger and selfishness and arrogance are dominating their life. They are

---

[1] Free downloads of the eBook are available at WCFAV.org. At the time of this writing, free downloads are also available at Barnes and Noble, Kobo, Smashwords, Apple iBooks, and other retailers.

miserable and unhappy because they allow addiction to harm their health.

Much is in the news these days about GABA[2] (relaxation), serotonin (happiness), dopamine (pleasure), and acetylcholine (learning and memory). God gave us billions of cells that communicate by sending chemical messages to the body, and these four neurotransmitters play a vital role. They control concentration, well-being, learning, stress, and more. Fascinating discoveries have been made about how important gut bacteria is (microbiome) to our overall health. Guess what leads to healthy neurotransmitters and gut bacteria? Yep, you guessed it—eating God-given foods and exercising build and maintain health and are essential to overcoming withdrawals.

Because of poor dietary choices, most people damage the communication between neurotransmitters. Ironically, withdrawals are often the result of the body rebalancing and normalizing these areas. God created serotonin to help us relax and dopamine for pleasure. When they are depleted and abused, recovery is a process that does not happen overnight.

Granted, I don't believe that everyone will be healthy. We live in a sinful world that often results in disease and sickness, but we can strive for health and take care of the wonderful gift of life. Inadequate nutrition affects us negatively in several different ways, and obesity and poor health lead to unproductivity.

I also encourage those suffering with depression and anxiety to look first at their spiritual and physical health. I'm not minimizing depression or anxiety, which can be debilitating,

---

[2] gamma-aminobutyric acid

but we shouldn't immediately assume that we need a prescription without first checking the obvious: Do we have a strong devotional and prayer life, are we monitoring our thought life and media choices carefully, are we taking care of our body, are we consuming foods that fuel anxiety or quench it? Yes, you read that right. Unhealthy food can alter norepinephrine and serotonin by affecting gut bacteria in negative ways. Those two natural chemicals play a huge role in mental health.

THE NEXT TIME YOU'RE TEMPTED, TRY ASKING, "DOES MY BODY NEED IT, OR DOES IT WANT IT?"

Consuming healthy, life-giving food is a constant challenge because temptation is always before us. The next time you're tempted, try asking, "Does my body need it—or does it want it?" If it needs it, consume it. If it wants it, think twice. It's generally not *if* poor nutrition causes damage but *when*. What a sad commentary on the lifestyle of a nation that has such great potential to live in the blessings God has so graciously given. Regardless of what the culture promotes, choosing to follow a healthier lifestyle is the first step in making health a priority (but not an obsession).

Another important step includes removing addictive substances that undermine health. This can be extremely difficult. A comment from a clinical nutritionist motivated me to discontinue my caffeine intake. He said that curbing caffeine leads to significant improvements in health, and he made the connection of depression, anxiety, and panic attacks to excessive caffeine.

As someone who once loved a few strong cups of coffee, I understand how hard it is. Most people can't go a few days without it; they're lucky to go a few hours. Caffeine intake in the form of energy drinks, soda, and coffee is highly addictive and damages health. The body is kept in a constant state of stress, resulting in adrenal fatigue. No wonder it breaks down often and many never overcome fatigue. Contrary to popular belief, stimulants don't actually help fatigue, they contribute to it by robbing Peter to pay Paul. The short-term results do not outweigh the long-term damage.

Since high levels of caffeine run along the same biochemical pathways in the brain as cocaine, opium, and amphetamines, quitting can be a nightmare. My suggestion is to back off day by day until intake is very minimal. Use organic green tea (light caffeine) whenever possible. You'll be shocked by the results. Granted, the first week to ten days may be torture, but it will be worth it. The withdrawal symptoms alone reveal the power of this drug. I was fascinated to learn that the logo of a very popular coffee franchise represents a seductive siren who allures and entices. How ironic.

Remember, your main goal is health, and stimulants aren't healthy. Ask yourself, "What is the risk versus the benefit to my health?" Will the benefits outweigh the risks? No. Your heart and organs work very hard, and they don't need added stress. As another example, some race cars are supercharged to run a quarter mile in seconds, but the engine must be replaced or at least repaired often. The same is true for your body; if you push it beyond where it's designed to go, performance won't last. The biblical approach is to take the safest route, not the fastest.

It's not my intent to point solely to coffee, stimulants, soft drinks, and energy drinks because there are many other addictive substances. Neither is being legalistic my goal. My heart is to simply share how the most addictive substance in America affects health, then let you be the judge.

Supplements to Offset Withdrawals

As always, consult your physician. Even healthy supplements can have some side effects, but in my opinion, what people commonly attribute to side effects from healthy supplements is just the body detoxifying from a harmful lifestyle. Because most people are not getting adequate amounts of nutrition, it's important to take quality supplements, especially when detoxing.

Many of the side effects associated with detox occur simply because the body is lacking nutrition in some area or trying to rebalance itself. A lack of vital nutrients can lead to fluctuating hormone levels, heart palpitations, anxiety, depression, and so on. Here are a few to consider, but keep in mind that these merely *complement* a healthy diet, not take its place. These can be costly—but so is poor health.

If finances are an issue, try taking them every other day after the first week to save on costs. My family does this often. I suggest buying these from a reputable company to avoid unhealthy fillers and binders.

Although many other supplements could be added to the list, this is my top ten:

1. **L-Glutamine.** This amino acid aids in muscle growth, immune support, and recovery and fights against inflammation and stress. I also encourage the use of complete and branch chain amino acids as well. They play a major role in healthy hormone levels as well as affect neurotransmitters.

2. **DL-phenylalanine.** This supplement plays a crucial role producing tyrosine. Tyrosine helps synthesize hormones, and we all know how important it is

to have hormones at the right levels. Men, did you know that alcohol and drugs significantly decrease testosterone, which in return, leads to mood swings, fat storage, and so on? This supplement can help, along with TDT-tribulus.

3. **5-Hydroxytryptophan (5-HTP)** is another important amino acid that the body uses to produce serotonin. This is critical for deep, healthy sleep and for overcoming depression and anxiety.

4. **Gamma-Aminobutyric Acid (GABA).** WebMD suggests that GABA may boost mood or have a calming, relaxing effect on the nervous system.[3]

5. **Concentrated trace mineral drops.** Since our body is severely lacking in these essential nutrients, add a few drops to water throughout the day. Serving-size directions should be on the back of the container. Make sure to drink plenty of clean water throughout the day as well.

6. **Raw whole food multivitamins.** Convenience-store vitamins often do not cut it. In this area, we need to purchase good vitamins that are not only absorbed better but also mimic real food. I would also add probiotics and extra vitamin E along with D3 and K2, which are often called the "dynamic duo" for their health benefits. I would also advise increasing vitamin C intake to a minimum of 1000 mg a day. Increase dosage throughout the day to aid in recovery.

---

[3] See more at "GABA (Gamma-Aminobutyric Acid)," WebMD, September 05, 2019, https://www.webmd.com/vitamins-and-supplements/gaba-uses-and-risks.

7. **Turmeric** is a high-powered anti-inflammatory that can help with arthritis and fighting disease.

8. **Resveratrol** is an antioxidant that helps fight disease by neutralizing free radicals. It can also lower blood pressure and ease joint pain.

9. **Omega-3, omega-6, and omega-9 fatty acids** are all important dietary fats.[4] I also add coconut oil to my diet but try not to consume too much oil. Instead, I eat the source it comes from such as nuts, avocados, and olives.

10. **Organic plant-based protein powder** can replace meals and will help get you back on track. I also occasionally add organic bone broth powder.

Additionally, I recommend eating organic colorful salads a few times a day using healthy salad dressing. When possible, I make my own dressing from healthy pepperoncini juice and homemade hummus. The key is to get the high fiber content of these foods, which moves the sludge out of the intestines during and after detox. Add organic beans for protein or a small organic chicken breast or drink a smoothie with it.

Organic vegetables and fruits are important because they (hopefully) don't contain harmful herbicides, fungicides, and pesticides. Just research the side effects of glyphosate for shock value. To properly detox, it's important to have your body working properly. I truly feel for the people who detox on chips, fast food, soda, energy drinks, and the like, which makes life much more difficult. In short, when you eat junk

---

4 More at https://www.healthline.com/nutrition/omega-3-6-9-overview.

food, you're introducing harmful substances back into your body as you're detoxing.

Have We Forgotten the Hidden Secret of Fasting?

Most of us have forgotten the hidden secret of fasting. Through fasting, our body becomes a servant instead of a master. When Jesus directs us, the outcome is always beneficial, spiritually and physically. Notice that He said, "When you fast" (Matthew 6:16). Scripture doesn't say, "When you sin" and "If you fast," but rather, "If you sin," and "When you fast." The obvious goal and benefit of fasting is spiritual, but there are physical benefits as well. Can we pray and seek God with all our heart with a headache, tight pants, and a sluggish, lethargic body strung out on our favorite addictive substance? Of course not. Does the way you feel affect your productivity and the quality of your life? Absolutely.

If we allow junk food and addictions to control our attitude and ability, it will hinder our fruitfulness for God. When we're always dealing with stress, anxiety, and sickness, can we do much for God? No, we will be limited. Granted, there are those who, through no fault of their own, have a debilitating illness. I'm assuming the reader understands that I'm speaking to those who can make changes.

What you put in the mouth (body) and the mind (soul) affects the spirit, and when you feed the spirit, it affects the body and the soul. I'm often asked to pray for people who have panic attacks, angry outbursts, and anxiety. That can be done, and God honors prayer, but are we opening the door to these issues by not halting highly addictive substances? Or are we renewing our mind by meditating on the Word and spending time in prayer? The physical affects the spiritual, and the spiritual affects the physical. Much of the healing I have witnessed over the years was the result of renewed stewardship of the body. We know that many emotions such as anger, bitterness, and jealousy are toxic to the body. Health also involves healthy emotions. Having a forgiving, loving, joy-filled heart does wonders for the body.

Again, I'm not suggesting that health should replace God and prayer, but it should complement them as we steward the gift of health. No one is perfect, but we are called to discipline our bodies and use wisdom. God does heal miraculously, even in our ignorance, but that shouldn't cause us to neglect our health. With almost fourteen million US children who are obese[5] and more than eleven million who are malnourished,[6] the need to address this topic has never been greater. Junk food is fueling the disease epidemic. Yet we pray for God to heal rather than ask for His help with the self-discipline to change harmful habits. What's wrong with this picture? "There are multitudes of diseases which have their origin in fullness and might have their end in fasting."[7]

The myth that fasting is bad for you is unfounded and has been disproved numerous times. Be careful when getting counsel from those who profit from that advice or who know little about how the body heals itself.

---

[5] "Childhood Obesity Facts: Prevalence of Childhood Obesity in the United States," Centers for Disease Control and Prevention, updated June 24, 2019, https://www.cdc.gov/obesity/data/childhood.html.

[6] "Facts about Childhood Hunger," No Kid Hungry, accessed October 11, 2019, https://www.nokidhungry.org/who-we-are/hunger-facts.

[7] James Morrison, quoted in Arthur Wallis, God's Chosen Fast (Fort Washington, PA: Christian Literature Crusade, 1977), 104–105.

Fasting sharpens spiritual insight, wisdom, and discernment. You're either controlling your body or your body is controlling you. We drive a certain way to pick up our addiction, we go to certain places because of our addiction, and we schedule things around our addiction. *Do we realize just how much our addictions control us versus us controlling them?*

Recall the scenario in chapter 4 about having lunch in a crowded mall. You and your family are famished from running errands. Just before leaving, you notice that your three-year-old is no longer with you—panic sets in! You must find your child at any cost. Are you going to eat first? Of course not. The passion to find your child is far greater than the desire to eat. That's exactly what fasting is: the desire to seek God is greater than the desire to eat.

Some may argue, "Fasting is too extreme!" Are we not living in extremely difficult times? Desperate times call for desperate measures. Dr. Caldwell Esselstyn reminds us about the other side of the coin: "Half a million people a year will have their chests opened up and a vein taken from their leg and sewn onto their coronary artery."[8] He calls that extreme, and so do I. We reap what we sow.

Recent statistics reveal that the opioid crisis is killing tens of thousands of people and alcoholism continues to ravish homes. Millions are walking away from their faith each year, marriages are in shambles, families are deteriorating, and suicide is an epidemic. I call that extreme! It's time that Christians get extreme in their warfare if they truly desire victory.

---

[8] Dr. Caldwell Esselstyn, quoted in Forks Over Knives, directed by Lee Fulkerson (Monica Beach Media, 2011).

> **WHEN GOD MOVES, PRAYER AND FASTING HAVE OFTEN BEEN THE CATALYST.**

A strong attack by the enemy requires a strong defense. When God moves, prayer and fasting have often been the catalyst.

Prepare yourself by getting the body and the mind ready. If possible, wean off everything that is hurting your health, both spiritual and physical. Most choices lead either to the filling of the Spirit or quenching and grieving Him. Giving in to one area of weakness lowers our defense in other areas.

Prayer, fasting, the Word, and worship starve the enemy's influence. As the flesh submits, we become more in tune with the things of God. A stagnant spiritual life turns into flowing waters. The mind becomes uncluttered and focused. The things of God, rather than the things of the world, begin to dominate our thinking.

Why wait? Procrastination keeps the car in neutral. You can't steer what's not moving; start the process of change today. An incident from the American Revolution illustrates the power of procrastination. It is reported that Colonel Rall, commander of the British troops in New Jersey, was playing cards when a courier brought an urgent message stating that General George Washington was crossing the Delaware River. Rall put the letter in his pocket and didn't bother to read it until the game was finished, but by then it was too late. His procrastination cost him the victory—and his life.

Begin today. You've probably fallen so many times that you have lost count—so have I. Don't focus on past mistakes. As a famous poem declares, "For all of life is like a race with ups and downs and all. And all you have to do to win is rise each time you fall."[9] God honors perseverance, not perfection.

As we close, don't forget one major theme of this book: Forget what lies behind and press ahead. Begin now initially or begin again. Success doesn't come without failure. It's through our failures that we learn how to succeed.

GOD HONORS PERSEVERANCE, NOT PERFECTION.

I want to challenge those who say they don't have the time to eat properly and exercise. We often forget just how precious time is. How many days, weeks, or even months do we waste because we don't prioritize our lives? We need to be very careful when we say that we don't have enough time. What we are really saying is that it's not important. If it were important, we would find the time. If we don't schedule time, time will schedule us. You'll never get everything done that "needs" to be done in the course of a day. Therefore, it's important to prioritize your day. Ask yourself, "What's the most important thing for me to do in any given hour?" In essence, it's all about leading a productive, balanced life and using time wisely. Don't let time be the excuse that stops you from succeeding.

Take it further:

- Check out the "Fasting Forum" on YouTube at https://www.youtube.com/watch?v=UWbV-A6lQxI&t=2329s.

---

[9] Attributed to Dr. D. H. (Dee) Groberg, "The Race."

- You can find my "Health Expo" on YouTube at: https://www.youtube.com/watch?v=xo_ScThDN0Y&t=6280s.

- Learn how to "Get Back on Track" can be found on YouTube at: https://www.youtube.com/watch?v=MKD1tmB9jl8&t=4560s

- For additional help in other areas, search for topical sermons at either WCFAV.org or ShaneIdleman.com.

Appendix 1

The Truth about Alcohol

True freedom in Christ allows for personal freedoms, but most freedoms are intended to work within a framework of social responsibility (Galatians 5:13). Food and beverage, for example, are good, but we are warned against extremes such as gluttony and drunkenness. Most anyone who has lived with these abuses understands why.

The person who consumes alcohol walks a very fine line between freedom and sin, responsibility and carelessness, liberty and abuse—overindulgence can even disqualify a person from leadership (1 Timothy 3). This discussion is not about a glass of wine or beer now and then; it's about abuse. Damage done to families and individuals demands a closer look. One correspondence I received stated, "I won't watch my kids be physically abused anymore. My husband's alcohol consumption is killing our family." Another person wrote, "Leaders in my church don't recognize that they are hurting people by abusing alcohol." One man said, "My wife has co-workers and parishioners fooled, but she is destroying our family from the inside out."

These are families and churches in crisis, all because liberty crossed the line. The demands of life often tempt us to seek gratification in alcohol and other things. We must be on high alert. The enemy uses "opportune times" to draw us away from God (Luke 4:13). The line is so thin that it is often hard to determine when we cross over. Personally, I believe that abstinence should be practiced by most Christians, especially if they drink often and in excess (these can be signs of alcoholism). This is especially true of leadership. The list of men and women who have lost a great deal due to alcohol is proof enough that liberty has limits. No one has lost anything by abstaining.

Jesus said that "wisdom is justified by all her children" (Luke 7:35). Does this liberty result in contentions, hurt feelings, negative comments, and questions about your drinking? Is it dividing friendships or causing unnecessary problems? This speaks for itself and can be early warning signs of alcoholism.

> THE LIST OF MEN AND WOMEN WHO HAVE LOST A GREAT DEAL BECAUSE OF ALCOHOL IS PROOF ENOUGH THAT LIBERTY HAS LIMITS. NO ONE HAS LOST ANYTHING BY ABSTAINING.

Alcohol abuse has created a sad commentary on the spiritual condition of the church. We often flaunt liberty and laugh in the face of God's grace. We use the opportunity to post our favorite beer brands and feature our favorite wines on social media, all under the guise of "exercising liberty." Be careful. Romans 14 has warnings in this area. Ironically, many use Romans 14 to support alcohol use, when the opposite is true: "It is better . . . not to do anything that will cause your brother or sister to fall" (v. 21 NIV).

Those who promote abstinence and avoid alcohol are often not "weak in the faith" (Romans 14:1), they are solid mature believers who have genuine concern. People who are weak in the faith are often those who abuse this liberty. It is the selfless motivation of love that keeps us from stumbling others. If love is not the motivation, a form of legalism may arise.

We all make mistakes, and a "holier than you" attitude is not the right approach. My intent is not to argue but to help those crossing the line. If this article upsets you, it might be an indication that change needs to take place.

If you continue to exercise this liberty, keep it private. A few years ago, I attended a conference where pastors were encouraged to meet at a pub after the general sessions. A few of these pastors could exercise their liberty, but why do so publicly? I wondered how many people at the conference stumbled because of it.

Social media influences on a broad scale. In Jesus's day, society was much more isolated—no Twitter, Instagram, or Facebook. We have no idea how many people are affected by social media. We can foster temptation just by the things we post.

Don't play with fire and walk into the enemy's camp. Liberties can easily become habits, and habits form addictions. Be honest. How much do you drink? Is it really one beer or a glass of wine now and then, or is it throughout the week and in large amounts? Is it a large goblet that holds three-fourths of a bottle of wine, which you fill twice? Ale beer, for example, often has two times more alcohol than normal beer. Having two ale beers may be the equivalent of four regular beers.

Do you make excuses in order to exceed moderation? Do you plan activities around alcohol? Do others comment on your drinking? Do you often argue and try to justify your position? Paul said that even though we have freedom, not everything is good for us. We should not become a slave to anything (1 Corinthians 6:12).

We are reminded in 1 Peter 2:16 that many use liberty to hide sin, as "a cloak for vice." If these points raise concerns, I encourage you to say, "Lord, I've been wrong. Remove my carnality, crush my pride, draw me closer to you. I repent of my sin and turn completely and unconditionally to you."

In our freedom, we can become a liability to ourselves, others, and the message of the gospel. It's often not *if* alcohol consumption causes damage but *when* it will cause damage. "Be very careful, then, how you live; not as unwise but as wise" (Ephesians 5:15 NIV).

Pastor John MacArthur states what many of us feel but seldom discuss: "It is puerile and irresponsible for any pastor to encourage the recreational use of intoxicants—especially in church-sponsored activities. The ravages of alcoholism and drug abuse in our culture are too well known, and no symbol of sin's bondage is more seductive or more oppressive than booze."[1] I couldn't agree more. The trend of young Christian leaders consuming alcohol on a regular basis is alarming. Many will look back and regret the damage that was done to lives and churches and to their own testimony.

Many counseling appointments are made because of alcohol and drug abuse. Add to that the number of domestic violence cases and children abused because of alcohol, and we would be remiss to ignore its dangers. Alcohol abuse, among

---

[1] John MacArthur, "Beer, Bohemianism, and True Christian Liberty," Grace to You, August 9, 2011, https://www.gty.org/library/blog/B110809#!.

other addictions, presents a sad commentary on the spiritual condition of the church today.

Consider the following:

The Bible never encourages crossing the line. With today's promotion and acceptance of alcohol, many easily cross the line. A preoccupation with alcohol is just one indicator of alcoholism; a preoccupation with drinking at events or social gatherings is another. Some even bring out their private collection of hard liquor after having a few drinks. This is not liberty but an addiction.

We assume that the alcohol content today is the same as in Jesus's day. In His day, water was often placed into the wine and thus decreased the alcohol content significantly (1 Timothy 5:23), much like an O'Doul's nowadays. Even many orthodox Jews in Israel today only have about 2 percent alcohol in their wine. "Strong drink" were drinks with higher alcohol content that led to drunkenness.

Some say, "Jesus ate and drank with sinners." John MacArthur again states, "But there is no suggestion in Scripture that Jesus purposely assumed the look and lifestyle of a publican in order to gain acceptance."[2] We should fellowship without engaging in the practices of a secular lifestyle. The world will know that we are Christians by our love and by our convictions, not by how well we imitate the world around us. We rarely hear non-Christians say, "I'm turned off by Christians because they seldom compromise." But we do hear, "Christians who say one thing and do another really turn me off." Guarding against compromise isn't just a good idea, it's

---

[2] MacArthur, "Beer, Bohemianism, and True Christian Liberty."

absolutely necessary when it comes to preserving our testimony. "Do not mix with winebibbers" (Proverbs 23:20).

"Jesus drank often." Not true. We find only purposeful incidents of Jesus having diluted wine over the course of three years, and not very often. Today, many Christians center everything around alcohol—fellowship, events, birthdays, and Bible studies. When alcohol is the center of attention, it becomes an idol and an addiction.

Jesus was filled with the Spirit. Holiness flowed from every area of His life. This cannot be said of those who consume alcohol regularly. What is the fruit of today's preoccupation with alcohol? Conversations often turn away from God, if they were there to begin with. We compromise our time and interests; we'd rather head to Vegas than a prayer meeting. The harmful fruit that results from a lifestyle focused on alcohol is proof enough.

In Jesus's day, society was much more isolated. We cannot calculate how many people are affected by today's social media. A person with five hundred "friends" may be encouraging dozens to stumble. It is the selfless motivation of love that keeps us from causing others to stumble (see Romans 14).

I recall a time when I was sent by someone to buy beer at a grocery store (I think we had family in town). Ironically, the cashier knew me. There were other times when I purchased a small amount of wine or beer. In each case, I felt convicted: *What if someone saw me?* You may say, "That's not a big deal," but for me it is a big deal because I'm a pastor, and people are watching. I went from the business world right into pastoring, and it took time to fully grasp this shift. I wish I could go back and handle those public interactions differently, but I can't. I can only learn from them and move forward. Remember, Galatians 5:13 tells us we should not "use our freedom to indulge the flesh."

In our freedom, we can become a liability to ourselves, others, and the message of the gospel. Why would we willingly walk into the enemy's camp?

Appendix 2

Depression and Mental Illness: 5 Things You Need to Know

The following article was published on September 16, 2019.

Many know all too well the debilitating effects of mental illness. We do a great disservice when we tell those struggling to "just get over it and think positive thoughts" or "read your Bible more." Although positive thinking (the right kind) is biblical, and it's crucial to meditate on God's Word, one cannot simply turn depression, anxiety, and hopelessness on and off like a light switch. But on the flip side, there are factors that contribute to mental anguish. After many years of praying with, talking to, and counseling thousands of people, I've found five factors that stand out that may cause mental pain. (Watch the short video here outlining these same points.[1])

1. Chemical imbalances and other physical factors can cause mental illness. Medication has a place, such as when neurotransmitters and hormone levels need assistance. In the same way that diabetes needs to be treated with insulin,

---

[1] See Shane Idleman, "Pastors and Christians Committing Suicide—What Is Going On?" on YouTube at https://youtu.be/dYsjHEqW52o.

some struggling with emotional pain may need medication, such as serotonin reuptake inhibitors, but medication doesn't always fix the problem. Often, it complicates it. Before jumping immediately on the medication bandwagon, consider the next four points. There isn't a one-size-fits-all approach, but we can look at a combination of things that may be adding to mental anguish.

2. The consequences of besetting sin can cause mental pain. In Psalm 32:3 (NASB), David said, "When I kept silent about my sin, my body wasted away through my groaning all day long." Ongoing unrepentant sin leads to mental anguish, depression, and anxiety. I'm not discounting deep emotional and psychological pain, but I do want to remind you that God makes provision for all our needs through a relationship with Him and obedience to His Word. Counseling with those skilled in the Word is invaluable and desperately needed, but all the counseling in the world will not work if the heart is not right. As a pastor, it would be highly inappropriate for me to neglect this point. If besetting sin or being out of God's will isn't the number one reason for mental pain, then it's a close second.

Again, I'm not suggesting that those who struggle with mental illness are engaged in sin—I hope that's not your takeaway—but unrepentant sin does lead to misery. For example, it was eventually revealed that two Christian leaders in my area who committed suicide were also engaged in extramarital affairs. And in the case of unbelievers, much of their depression, shame, and guilt is tied to the fact that they don't know God. Once repentance and trust in Christ take place, the enormous burden is lifted.

This is why pastors should preach repentance when God leads. *People need to be lovingly encouraged but also lovingly confronted from time to time.* Repentance is a beautiful word that reestablishes our relationship with God. We need to abort sin as soon as it's conceived (James 1:14–15). Sin has a life cycle—it either grows or withers, depending on whether we feed or starve it.

If you believe that your depression is being fueled by unrepentant sin, take time now and confess. God can restore and rebuild your life. If you're not sure where the depression is coming from, then spend time in prayer and reading God's Word. Ask Him to reveal blind spots that may have developed over time, or if there are other issues causing it. Many years ago, I heard an incredible sermon series from a pastor who struggled for years with depression. One day God showed him that he was too concerned about the size of his church and his reputation. He was also negative and critical. As soon as he repented and got his heart right, the depression lifted. It was an amazing testimony.

3. A toxic diet can affect mental health. No surprise here. What's eating you may have to do with what you're eating. Most people know that poor food choices affect *physical* health, but they fail to see the connection with *mental* health. Unhealthy food is a toxic choice when we factor in growth hormones, antibiotics, GMOs, drug residue, pathogens, biotoxins, chemicals, and carcinogens that wreak havoc on our bodies. Poor food choices cause a severe lack of vitamins and minerals that actually stabilize our emotions; this lack plays a huge role in mental instability. For example, if you read this book you learned that the *Diagnostic and Statistical Manual for Mental Disorders* lists caffeine-related disorders such as caffeine intoxication, caffeine-induced anxiety disorder, and caffeine-induced sleep disorder that lead to depression, severe anxiety, and extreme irritability. If we believe that we can drink a high-powered stimulant day in and day out and not have it affect our health, we are gravely mistaken. The same is true with alcohol. It's a powerful depressant. Both caffeine and alcohol harm physical and emotional health, as well as prevent deep healing sleep.

This then begs the question, "How many are suffering mentally and physically simply because of poor health—continuing the addiction rather than removing the cause of the problem?" For example, type 2 diabetes is a diet-related disease. Did you catch that? Type 2 is caused by our diet. Not in all cases but in most, depression, anxiety, irritability, and the like could be severely curtailed if health (spiritual and physical) was a priority. Ironically, a lack of sleep is very common in those with high anxiety. Do you see a connection here? Sadly, even when I share this information, very few want to change.

Many Christians reference Charles Spurgeon's depression. No one knows what caused it, but after poring over his biographies, I'm left with the impression that physical health was not a priority. How do we know that this didn't play a role in his depression and gout? Gout is caused by excessive uric acid in the blood, often fueled by certain foods. Spurgeon was an incredible preacher, and physical health should not be our main priority, but we should not overlook the health of our bodies when we can.

We were created to consume living, life-sustaining, God-given foods that nourish and support a healthy body, not dead, life-depleting food from a factory. The life of the food is to be deposited into the body to support and maintain life and health. Ironically, when food is withheld, as in the case of fasting, healing often follows. Dr. Yuri Nikolayev, a psychiatrist at the University of Moscow, treated schizophrenics with water fasts for twenty-five to thirty days. This was followed by eating healthy foods for thirty days. Seventy percent of his patients remained free from symptoms for the duration of the six-year study. The health benefits of fasting are incredible. (For more help in this area, download my book, *Feasting and Fasting*, for free here.[2])

4. A demonic attack can affect mental health. As stated in the book, we can't rule out the possibility of a spiritual attack. Throughout the New Testament, demonic activity caused mental anguish. If a person takes high-powered drugs, they may only increase the problem and could open the door to further demonic activity. *Pharmakeía* (from where we get our word *pharmacy*) means to administer drugs. In the Bible, it was often tied to the practice of magic and sorcery. Medication for depression can cause suicidal thoughts. It's an area we need to be careful in.

How do you know if an attack is demonic? Take it to God in prayer and fast for a day. Read the next point and see if your spiritual diet is playing a role. Ask for wisdom and deliverance if necessary. Have you opened any obvious doors such as palm reading, tarot cards, alcohol, drugs, or Ouija boards? Is there a family history of occult practices? Have those strong in the faith pray for you regularly. *Sometimes strongholds have to be pulled down one brick at a time.* Saturate your mind in the Word, and pray and worship throughout the day.

---

[2] https://shaneidleman.com/books.

Satan also looks for open doors from our past. Just this week I spoke to a young man who struggled with anxiety from a very young age. Medication didn't fix it; meditating on God's Word did. He realized that the stronghold took a tight grip when his parents divorced, leaving the influence of a broken home at a young age. Only a renewed mind and prayer against this stronghold delivered him.

5. An unhealthy spiritual diet negatively affects mental health. What are you feeding your mind? Are you fueling fear and paranoia by spending too much time listening to the media? Are you watching horror movies—especially paranormal and excessively violent ones—and ungodly entertainment? What kind of music do you listen to—uplifting and encouraging or worldly and sensual? Take time and read Philippians 4 to see what the apostle Paul has to say about our mental diet. What you put into your mind plays a huge role in your mental health. If you have a lot of time for entertainment but no time for God, mental health will suffer. The most difficult challenge for me as a pastor is witnessing the tragic results of people dying spiritually because of the choices they are making. Many are sowing to the wind and reaping the whirlwind by not putting God first.

I'm writing this last paragraph as I'm preparing for a memorial service for someone who took their own life. Suicide hurts those closest to you; the pain lasts a lifetime. It's one of the cruelest things we can do to those we love, especially if children are involved. The guilt for family members can be unbearable.

If you find yourself trapped in addiction, misery, and depression, there is hope. God continually calls us back to Him. If you return with all your heart, He will return to you. That's a gift of the greatest value . . . a promise that will never fail. He is our only Hope. But if you've done that and have a vibrant relationship with God, yet still struggle, keep pressing on. Bouts of depression are common to most of us as a by-product of this fallen world, but the reward at the end of the race will far exceed the disappointments of this world. Don't give up . . . look up!